WITHDRAWN

Puzzled America

OTHER BOOKS
BY SHERWOOD ANDERSON

Puzzled America

By
Sherwood Anderson

PAUL P. APPEL, *Publisher*

MAMARONECK, N.Y.

1970

TO

ROGER SERGEL

Contents

Introduction

THE sketches, attempts at pictures of America now, here being made into a book are the result of a good deal of wandering about. I have tried to be as impersonal as I could.

I am in the position of most writers nowadays. Formerly, for a good many years, I was a writer of tales. It may be that I should have remained just that, but there is a difficulty. There are, everywhere in America, these people now out of work. There are women and children hungry and others without enough clothes. Middle-aged men and women, who but a few years ago felt themselves secure, are now suddenly facing old age, thrown out of their security. They have been thrown out of their houses, off their farms. You see and talk with such people. The amazing thing to the observer is that there is so very little bitterness.

People want to tell their stories, are glad to tell. I blame myself that I do not get more of these stories, do not often enough get the real feeling of the people to whom I talk.

I am caught up in something in which all present-day writers are caught. Well, not all. There are some of our writers—they may be the wise ones —who keep themselves in the clear. Such a one says to himself, "What have I to do with all this? We writers know that government has gone on for a long time. There never was such a thing as a just government."

This is all very well but there is a sort of blindness, too. I cannot take the impersonal tone. It will not do any more. Government has again grown near to life. It may be that the politicians remain a race apart but the politicians are no longer the government. It may even happen that presently they will get lost.

You, the reader, must imagine the writer as going about, constantly puzzled as you are. Let us say I am in the house of a friend. He may be a well-to-do man. He is at bottom a kindly man.

But he is prosperous. Let us say he is a man this long depression has not very much touched. There are a good many such people. I am told that during the very worst of the depression, during the winters of nineteen thirty-one and two, the sale of the more expensive luxuries of life went right on.

There are the extravagant ones, the money-spenders, but who wants to stop them? Where would we writers, painters, sculptors, etc., be if there were no people ready to throw money away? You, the reader, if you have bought this book of mine, cannot eat it, you cannot convert it into clothing. You may burn it but it will not much warm your house, if you have a house.

Why, we writers do not want to put an end to extravagant living. We want more of it. "Hurrah!" we cry. "Let every one live extravagantly."

Women be beautifully garbed. Men walk freely and proudly through the streets.

If the American writer chances to be a good deal of a wanderer, as I am, he is constantly struck by something. He becomes more and more convinced of the vast richness of America. Of the waste of wealth here, the waste of land, of potential power in coal and oil, in vast unneeded buildings. How our forests have been wasted, the power in our streams wasted, the land itself wasted.

Why, it should be a proud country, filled with well-fed, beautifully housed men, women, and children.

And there is all this nonsense about there being no work for workmen. Ye gods! What ugly houses, what ugly towns I have seen in my travels these last few years! Could we not begin to build America? It needs it. We speak of our modern conveniences. How many of our people have them? Why there is work here for all men for a hundred years.

What is wrong? Why can't we do it? The capitalists? Is it not true that there will always be strong men? What is the real difference between Stalin of Russia and, let us say, the elder Morgan? If we really got a new set-up here, would not exactly the same sort of men be in power? Who cares?

I am spending the evening in the house of a well-to-do man. He made his money, let us say, during the time of Coolidge but he escaped the disaster that came later. A good many people did escape. I have been talking with this man, have been spending the evening with him and we have been talking of government, of unemployment. Of what else do men speak nowdays? It comes into every conversation. What's going to happen? What about Roosevelt? Will he make good? Will he go to the right or to the left?

When it comes to the rich or the well-to-do man, he thinks secretly what Americans have always thought. Isn't this the land of opportunity? "You look at me. I began as a poor boy. I made good." He doesn't say that. He does imply that there is a good deal of nonsense about all of this poverty, and I go out of his house wanting to take the man with me on my wanderings. "Come on," I want to say to him, "let's go look."

It is not unlikely that in leaving such a man's house—it has happened to me—this would be after dark at night—I see a man lurking in an open place between two buildings. I stop and look. He is pawing over the contents of a garbage can. It does happen, things like that, to Americans, people in this big rich place. It happens that men have no shoes, that men here who have families go home at night to hungry, crying children, to sordidness, to cheap, unhealthy living, and it is not true, dear reader, that these men, these Americans, are necessarily in any way inferior to you or to me.

It is a bit odd, isn't it, dear reader, that the American cry, "Make good! Make good!" that we all heard when we were boys—that I dare say boys are still hearing—that it so often leads to a kind of blindness. I know. At various times in my life I have been prosperous. I have made some money, have good clothes, a car, a warm house. I have been that way and I have been broke, and always, for some curious reason, I have always, when broke, been more alive to others, more aware of others.

But is there any necessity for any one's being broke in a land like this? It is so rich. That is the big fact I have got out of all my wanderings these last few years—all of this travelling in the midst of the depression—a growing sense of the fact of the vast wealth of the country itself. I want other men to be rich so that if by chance riches come to me I may be comfortable about it. I want every one to be extravagant so that I may be at ease in my own extravagance.

It happens that, a few years ago, I was in a certain house, in a certain American town, at a very sad time. I was there because I admired rather tremendously the man of the house, my friend. He was very ill and was not expected to live. He did live but there was a certain afternoon when his death was expected at any moment.

He was a man deeply loved by those about him, a cultured, kindly, intelligent man. At the crisis of his illness I was at the house and went into the back yard. There was a little arbor and I went to sit in it, and presently my friend's two daughters came out of the house. They walked down the back steps of the house and stood together near the arbor. They looked stunned and for a time stood thus in silence, and then one of the daughters, the older one, took the hand of her sister. "If I could only believe in God," she said. "If we could both believe."

"It would be such a comfort if we could both kneel here on the grass and pray—if we could believe."

The two sisters stood looking at each other, the tears running down their cheeks, but they did not pray, at least not aloud. They stood for a moment and then, with the stunned look in their eyes and the tears still flowing, went back into the house.

And so, there it is—"If I could believe. I want belief." It is a kind of cry going up out of the American people. I think it is about the absolute net of what I have been able to find out about Americans in these last few years of travelling about, in all of this looking at people and talking to them.

"I want belief, some ground to stand on. I do not want government to go on just being a meaningless thing. I do not want life to be so stupid—so silly."

We are people who passed through the World War and its aftermath. We saw the upflaring of prosperity, lived through the Harding and the Coolidge times. We got the hard-boiled boys and the wise-crackers. We got, oh, so many new millionaires. As a people now we are fed up on it all.

We do not want cynicism. We want belief.

Can we find it in one another, in democracy, in

the leadership we are likely to get out of a democracy?

I think that these sketches of people, as I have found them, living and working, or out of work and for the time down and out—they should at least show that there is belief here that we can. There is a willingness to believe, a hunger for belief, a determination to believe. If the leaders we, as a democracy—and we are still a democracy, very much a democracy—if the leaders we are now throwing up into places of power do not lead along new roads, if they fail us, the failure will not be due to a lack of belief. We have got this rich land and this people rich with this new hunger for belief. The outstanding, dominant thing now in almost all of the Americans I have been seeing is this new thing, this cry out of their hearts for a new birth of belief.

In the South

At the Mine Mouth

At the Mine Mouth

I AM writing from the coal-mining country. There is too much to tell. On every side of me there are stories. The stories look at me out of the eyes of men and women. They shout at me. I should not be writing in this way. I should stay here in one of these shacks in this coal-mining town. I should know for a long time these men, women, and children. Why do I hurry from town to town?

America is too vast. There are too many stories to tell.

I remember how my brother-writer, the Englishman, D. H. Lawrence, spoke of his own English coal-mining people. He was a sensitive and a hurt man and I think he came to hate his English miners. They were on the surface too rough, too brutal for him. He remembered too well his own father. Most men do. He spoke of his English Midland miners as heavy, inert men. They went leering down English mining-town streets filled, he thought, with hatred. I do not feel hatred here among our American miners.

I keep asking questions:

"How is the NRA working out?"

"What the hell?"

"Not so swell."

It is like a song——

"What the hell?"

"Not so swell."

I am at the edge of a coal-mining town. I was last here two years ago. When I was here then there was a strike raging. There was a battle. This whole mining country is an old battle ground. Here that battle was fought—there another battle. Long rifles poked out from among rocks up in the hills. Men pitching forward dead. These men know death intimately—above ground and below ground. When I was last here mine guards stood about everywhere—"thugs." The mine guards, formerly employed by the mine owners, were called "thugs" by the miners. There was bitter hatred between the miners and the so-called "thugs," but there was respect. I visited a battlefield where the miners once shot it out with the mine guards. A one-armed miner talked to me of an old battle.

"They got four of us, but before we got through we got over one hundred of them," he said. "They didn't quit. They fought it out with us. If any one ever tells you that these thugs haven't the guts, you tell them they don't know the mines."

Two years ago the "thugs" were at the entrances

to the town. They stood everywhere on the streets of the town. There were towns, whole counties, down in this coal-mining country that you, being an outsider, could not enter without first submitting to search. There had been battles fought. Men were being killed. Miners, with their long squirrel rifles, were even then lying in the hills.

It should be borne in mind—I do not believe it is generally known—that every official over at Harlan, Kentucky, where so short a time ago miners were daily being killed by officials, kept in office, it was openly proclaimed, by the mine owners— admittedly servants of the mine companies—the workers everywhere denied the right to organize —meetings broken up—labor leaders shot, beaten up, driven out of the counties—at Harlan, Kentucky, every official involved in the recent war between the miners and the workers has been swept out of office. It is significant, I think, that in many of these towns, into which came the Communists, often fighting men like the miners, Communists ready to go to jail, to be shot, the miners loved the Communists, who came to fight with them and for them without at all understanding the Communist philosophy.

"The NRA—hell, it isn't working so good." That is the verdict. There are plenty of chiselers

7

—the chiselers being spotted just the same. "We have got to get our union stronger before we can help the government take care of the chiselers."

I am writing this letter from the pit's mouth at the edge of a mining town. The man who has been driving me through the mining country now stands over there within sight, talking to a group of miners. In spite of the NRA there are thousands of miners not yet re-employed. Mines are standing unworked. There are too many mines, too much coal. Men everywhere are still out of work. There is grim poverty here. It is a cold bleak day but, in the field here, at the edge of the mining town, there are bare-legged miners' children running around. The lips of the children are blue with cold. They are ragged. They look underfed. These American children are members of a vast army of American undernourished children.

In the land of plenty—in the land of milk and honey.

Miners' wives go in and out of little shacks. These miners' wives lose their beauty early. There has been hard-bitten life going on for years in this country.

It is a country of vast wealth. Millions have been drawn out of American earth. There are great lakes of oil under the ground. Gas spurts up, and down in the ground are untold millions of tons of bedded coal—untouched as yet. It is a country of vast water power—the land also of the new white coal.

The men I see there, straggling across the streets of a mining town, in sight there—gathering in groups by the company store——

There are growls, oaths, outbreaks of profanity. These are fighting men.

"Sure, I am in debt. I am at work now, but they pay me in nothing but scrip. We haven't had anything in our house but a little fat pork and some beans. For fat pork they charge me nineteen cents in the company store, but if I had money I could buy it at nine cents a pound in one of the free stores."

The reds have been in here. A young Communist girl came.

"What did she want?"

"She seemed to want, most of all, to get into jail."

A young miner spoke to me. "Sure," he said, "when the reds come in here we listen to them. We give 'em a cheer. A lot of things the reds say are true.

"We believe in them as we believe in the preachers when we go to church," he said. "The preachers tell us about Heaven. We like to hear it all right, but it doesn't seem to have much to do with what we are up against, right now, down here in these coal-mining towns."

I have been curious to know whether or not there is, in the minds of these workers, a growth of the fascist idea—the state drawn up into the figure of one man—the individual becoming magnified through identification with the great one—great Italy—great Germany—but I do not believe that there is, in the men and women I have been talking with, any notion at all as yet of the great America—America *über alles*. There is in the average American a profound humbleness. Everywhere there is uncertainty. "I have been living for a long time in one house, but the lease has expired. I must move into a new house. What will it be like?" Our sense of humor is not dead. In all my talks with American men met at street corners, with workers, farmers, and with the miners down in this country I am now in, I have heard nowhere, from the lips of any man or woman, any talk at all of the great overshadowing destiny of America. The Fascisti thing is not yet in the minds of the average American. We are still at heart a democracy. A hunger to do the thing together in some way is still alive in us.

During the last week I have been here in the coal fields. I have been talking to newspapermen of the back country, to small hillside farmers, to miners with their lamps in their caps, met at the pit's mouth.

The feeling in the country is not yet revolution. There must be a revolution in feeling before there can be a revolution in fact. What men are saying to themselves is something like this:

"If some one man can go through with it—a Roosevelt or some other—if he can lead us into something new—the workers having a real chance —if he can do this without terror of revolutions— it's worth a shot, isn't it?"

"We would not expect him to come through to perfection. If he would but lead us along the road far enough so that we know that our feet are upon the road—that at last we are going somewhere."

"If some leader could do that it would be enough now. New men would arise—in the states —in the counties—in the towns—in the cities."

"Let's give this democracy thing another whirl yet."

"There is at least a chance to set up the framework of a new thing. Be quiet. Wait! Don't push. Those who have had a strangle hold upon America have been served long enough."

The above are sentences jotted down. They are the meat of what I have been hearing. They are the thoughts, come from the lips of Americans talked to in the back country during this week.

There is a feeling running through the ranks of labor. Everywhere in the mining country I have sensed it, felt it, heard it on the lips of miners: "We've got to have a chance."

A realization everywhere among the workers of the rottenness of many of the old unions. "Sure," they say, "the grafters had us on the run. The bosses had us whipped."

There is a quiet faith—not necessarily in the super-man.

Everywhere this new hope. A door has been jerked open. "Some day, soon now," a miner said to me, "it will no longer be a disgrace to call yourself a worker here in America.

"The other ones—the old ones in politics—used to talk so big to us. They talked of the nobility of labor and then they took all the nobility out of it. They made a dog of you, a slave. Man after man did it. It has been going on now for a long, long time."

"And now?"

Hesitancy. Laughter in the midst of poverty.

Curses thrown at the heads of local relief agencies, cries of politics, of graft, graft, graft.

"When it comes to politics most of us are like hogs rooting in the woods for acorns. That goes for nearly all of us, the blacks and the whites. When there are plenty of acorns we get fat, and when there ain't any acorns we starve. We've had our eyes on the ground. We never have looked up to see where the acorns come from."

The speaker was a Negro coal miner. He was also a preacher. I had come down the road to his shack in an open field in a car driven by a one-legged miner. The Negro miner was a man who had been thrown out of a mining town because of a strike.

Pegleg, my driver, knew every man, woman, and child along the valley. He had been a Socialist office holder in the district. Once he was an official of the United Mine Workers. I had got him because he was so widely known in the mines. He took me to the Negro coal miner who was also a preacher. "You get a car and drive me," I said to him. "I'll give you a day's work." He had a cork leg, his own leg having been lost in the mines. He had to reach down with his two hands, lift the dead leg and place it on the clutch.

13

We went to little mining towns.

We went up little creeks.

We forded creeks.

We talked to miners, to miners' wives, to miners' daughters.

We met groups of miners coming out of the mines at evening in the little dirt roads that come down from the hills, the lamps burning in their caps, the alive eyes of rough, alive men looking out from blackened faces. It was difficult to tell the white workers from the blacks. Many Negroes have come in here. They do not push them out of the mine workers' unions. In the mines the blacks and whites work together. "A man's a man," the Negro, who is also at times a preacher, had said to me.

The Negro miner was a man who could not get work any more. It was because he was known as a fighter. "He's a trouble-maker," they told me. He explained his situation to me, laughing as he talked. "They gave me a physical examination," he said. "It was a way of shoving me out. They told me I was too old to work in the mines, that I was N. G. They told me to go on relief.

"To hell with relief!" he said. "I don't want no man's relief. A man's a man," he said.

The Negro miner was husky. He rolled up his

sleeves to show me the muscles of his brawny arms. "I'm a miner, but I'm a preacher too," he said. "I know about God." He had a simple and a grand faith. My mind keeps going back to the Negro man, met here in the mine country. I liked him. "You take a look at me," he said. He did not seem to hold it against the mine owners that they were aware of the danger in him and in his kind. He had built himself a little shack in a field at the edge of the mining town from which he had been ejected. There was a stove made out of an iron tar barrel he had picked up on the road. The wind whistled through his shack.

The one-legged man driving my car had turned out of the highway, forded a creek, and pulled up at what was called a tent colony. All in the colony were dispossessed miners.

The place was like an old battlefield. It was that. When we had got into the field and had stopped the car before a little cluster of tents and shacks—sagging tents now—torn tents—patched tents—from where we stood, after we got out of the car—the one-legged man had to lift his leg out of the car and steer it straight before he let himself go, to half fall out of the car—from where the car stood we could look up the valley to a mining town.

In the long valley—the hills going straight up on either side of the towns are like some queer disease broken out on the body of Mother Earth. The towns give you that feeling, of disease, of a diseased civilization.

The thought's in me: that in America—here in this place of infinite wealth—men, women, and children should live like this.

"And they say there is no work to be done; they talk of the fear of leisure.

"There could be work here, for all the men in this valley for a hundred years, making it a man's country, a woman's country, a child's country."

As I had been driven down the valley, through town after town, stopping to go into mining company stores, talking to men, to Jim and Frank and Joe and Tom.

New towns.

Old towns.

Here is a place where a booming mine town stood ten, fifteen, twenty years ago. Now the town is in ruins. Cabins are sagging on their rickety foundations. There is a black dust over everything. Mine tipples and mine runways, that carried coal roaring down to freight cars, are falling into black decay.

I had ridden down the valley saying to myself

under my breath—"In this place, civilization has become a disease. The towns are disease towns."

I had been looking up into the hills and down to the gray-green river flowing down into the valley. There is oil and gas in the valley. There is salt down in the earth. Great chemical factories have come in. There is coal. Untold millions of tons of black coal have been jerked up out of the ground.

After all these twenty, thirty, fifty years of mining the men of the valley tell you laughing— "We haven't touched it, we haven't scratched it," they say. As you ride down the valley men tell you that you are driving over great seams of untouched coal, this far down below the earth surface. "We have only taken some, a little of it, out of the hills where the shaft can be run straight in."

"We haven't touched it."

"It's here."

"There's power, lying asleep here in this valley, to run half America."

Pride in brotherhood, in the buried wealth of the land, local pride, town pride struggling to live —even in the poor little mining towns. There is something pathetic and at the same time magnificent in these men, the coal miners of America, in a certain something very hard to express but very real in them. It may be simple love of manhood in self and in other men. I think there is in them something of the American pioneer. There is something distinct and real separating them now from the defeated factory hands of the cities. They are not defeated men. Of all the American workers I have been among, they are closest to the lumber-jacks.

Like the lumberjacks, the miner does not work in gangs. The axe man of the lumber camp works with one other man. He is in direct contact with nature. A great tree is to be felled and it is of overwhelming importance that the man working with you, your partner, your brother man, be a man of cool judgment, that he be a man courageous and alive. A false swing of the moving axe and down the tree comes on you, crushing out your life. Look up your family history. What great-grand-father of your own was killed by a falling tree?

And it's so also in the mines. The two men, the miners, go back along the shaft to the room where they are to take out coal. Now days they lay down their own tracks, back into the room where they are cutting out the coal. They make the undercut, they put in the shot, they fire the shot, they shovel the coal into the mine cars. Partitions have to be left between the rooms and wooden props must be put up. Always there is danger. A little carelessness, a sag, and down the roof comes. Every day in the mine men are crushed under thousands of tons of slate.

One of the mining men said to me—"One of these days," he said, "just for fun, we'll have a parade down through the valley. We'll go through the towns. We'll go through the cities. It will be a parade of the victims of the mines, of the cripples, of the blind, of the one-legged, of the one-armed. We can get them out of almost every house in every mining town, out of almost every mining family.

"The figures of the dead crushed in the coal. We'll put dummies on trucks to represent the dead.

"We should take the parade to New York, to Chicago, to Washington. We should parade before Congress. We should show them what it costs to tear the coal out of these hills."

I go back to the Negro miner who, because he is a trouble-maker, a natural leader, cannot work any more. As I was coming out of his shack, where we had been sitting, talking of coal mining in Alabama, in Kentucky, in Tennessee—he had been a wandering miner, a drifter like myself. He had been a wandering preacher——

19

"I mine when I get a chance," he said. "I preach the word of God when I get a chance."

"We have been like hogs rooting in the woods for acorns," he said. "We have had our eyes on the ground but now we are beginning to look up."

"We are going to try to find out where the acorns come from."

"We are beginning to look up."

"If we do not make good some day it is our fault," the Negro miner shouted to me as I drove away down the valley.

The Price of Aristocracy

The Price of Aristocracy

IT is intangible and illusive—this feeling for the South and all it stands for. You have it or you haven't. You can't put your finger on what arouses it in you. It must be born in you or come down into you from a grandfather or a grandmother. Each of these Southern States has its own individuality but there also is this other thing, the Southland. Well, she isn't perfect. She is opinionated, headstrong, not so beautiful now. But you adore her. I spoke of this feeling to a Virginia woman, of one of the so-called "first families." She hadn't travelled much.

"You Virginians," I said, "what do you know of the South?"

Shades of Robert E. Lee and Stonewall Jackson! She looked at me with intense scorn in her eyes. She became almost vulgar.

"What? You Yank!"

I was thinking of the lower South, of the interior South. Since I was a boy I have been coming down here. It may be that the feeling, the hunger, got into me through my father. He fought on the Northern side in the Civil War, having gone North from North Carolina, before the war—an intellectual conviction with no heart in it had, I suspect, got him in——

My own first trip South was on freight trains—bumming down through Kentucky, Tennessee, into Georgia, east to Charleston. The other bums on the trains kept warning me. "Look out for these interior Southern towns. They'll nab you and sell you out—to work on one of their chain gangs." Obvious cruelty of all Southern peoples, in me too. I understood vaguely.

I came back North, took up the Northern civilization—onward and upward—had my spells of being thoroughly sick of it, chucked it, went South again. I remember my first trip South as a mature man. No Florida beaches for me. I had, for five years, been at work in Chicago. You know the motto of Chicago. "I Will."

"You will what?"

I had, for all of the five years, been so in earnest, working in the daytime, studying at night.

"I'll be a big man. Look out for me. I'm going to be a big one."

A sudden sickness, inside. I had saved a little money. I went to Mobile.

Why Mobile, I didn't know. I had never heard of any one going there as I went. I was like the

New York man I once met living in Selma, Alabama. He had settled down there, on a river bank.

"Why Selma?"

"I don't know. I just bought a ticket."

I intended to loaf, smell, taste, see, feel. Is there an American man of the so-earnest North who doesn't understand the hunger? This American theory of life, like the Hebrew theory, that a man must make good at something, justify his existence, make two blades of grass grow where but one grew before—there is a side to me, as to most men, that has always cried out, "It's nonsense."

There are too many blades of grass, too much cotton, corn, and tobacco.

"Produce! Produce!" Is that all we know? I went to Mobile—had very little money. "All right," I said. I had been consorting with moneyed men, trying to learn their ways. I hadn't found them so likable. "You'll have to live frugally," I told myself. You can do it in the South. Most of the nice Southerners I've known were poor.

I stayed one night, after my arrival, in a hotel and then found a room in what had evidently once been an aristocratic section. The rich are always moving, getting a "better address." That's what gives us wanderers our chance. The old house into which I moved had fallen into decay but you don't mind decay so much—in the South. I got a huge old room with high ceilings and cockroaches and a balcony that looked out over Mobile Bay.

Warm days of doing nothing—loafing on my balcony—listening to voices in Mobile streets—soft voices of both whites and Negroes. I went to walk in warm January rains, walked on the docks to look at foreign ships come for cotton—took up-river steamers—they still had them then—and went far into the interior. I got to know mates, captains, and pilots of little dirty river steamers.

What t'ell? What's your hurry? That's it—to learn to take it in, through the senses—the Negroes do it naturally, bless'em—the warm sunshine—the clean, sweet smells in the piney-woods country, east of Mobile, the beauty of the Southern soil, the red country.

There are three big rivers which come down to make Mobile Bay and they all come down out of the red country. The red soil washes down, in the spring rains, into the bay. I have seen Mobile Bay, in late March, after the heavy spring rains, when I have stood over on the eastern shore on the Fair-hope side, when it was almost blood red under the evening sun.

The American South should be America's garden spot. It should be one of the very lovely lands of the world.

The land has been abused, terribly abused.

I have had times of hating the old families of the South, the so-called "old aristocracy." They were—must have been—oddly separated from the land itself. If you set up as an aristocracy, that's the price you pay. You are bound to be separated from the land itself, if you do not work the land yourself, with your own hands. Some of these old Southern families, the rich, slave-owning old families, went straight across the South, destroying the land as they went. Their story is the story of the lumber barons of the North. Thirty million acres of worn-out land in the State of Georgia alone. Read the old story of the agricultural South. Forget for the moment about magnolias and moonlight.

The question, a fair one—Can I make any claim at all to aristocracy, if I do not respect the ground under my own feet? If I wear out a piece of land, move on to a second piece and wear that out—thinking only of money to be made from the land—in what way do I differ from any money-minded man? I take it you can't be money-minded, profit-minded and lay claim at the same time to being an aristocrat.

There is too much aristocracy talk, based on money, in America now. To be sure you can't condemn the entire old land-owning South in this way. That's what stops any man who sits down to write a blast on a class. Some stuck, loved their places, loved a particular valley, hillside, river bottom, old house.

It has to be remembered that only a few Southerners ever owned slaves. There was always a great class, the economic underdogs—whites, I mean—that had no slaves or lost them, had no land or lost it. The class grew, just as we all have seen the dispossessed class grow all over America, under modern industrialism.

And here is a confusion, too. There always is great talk of family in the South and you would think hearing the talk, that the Poor Whites, Hill Billies, Georgia, and Florida Crackers, that these poor people, little tenant farmers of the South, share-croppers, so often ignorant, shiftless, beaten—the children undernourished or poorly nourished—they, the ones so often back of Southern lynchings—trying to assert superiority to something—you would think sometimes, hearing the talk, that these people were of some inferior stock. It isn't true. Often they bear proud old names. They got beaten in the economic struggle. That's the plain, simple story.

And they paid.

Whole generations of white men, their wives, daughters, sons—pretty much outside the modern world, the things we Americans brag of, mechanical development of life, education, warm clothes, good clean housing, modern machinery to do most of the old brutalizing labor.

Going South sometimes, I have gone into the upper South, sections of Tennessee, Virginia, North and South Carolina, upper Georgia, where the cotton mills have come in, and have written, damning what I have seen there in the old days—not so old, either—little children in the mills at twelve, tired women working all night—the intense speed of the modern machines, nerve exhaustion——

Often, to me, extreme beauty of the machinery itself. What has seemed to me some of the best writing I have ever done has been about machines —the intense, swirling, colorful beauty of some of these mills. I have wanted poets to go into the factories, painters to go in——

That curious contrast, the care lavished on the machines, the carelessness about human lives.

Myself fighting it out with some factory owners

—some of them honest, keen men—I have, more than once, walked half a night talking with some such man——

Competition with other mills. It seems to be true in every industry—one greedy man can throw a whole industry out of gear. They all go in to compete in the same markets.

And in the South something else not so much known in Northern towns. At least, in the country surrounding most of the Northern towns that became industrial, there wasn't worn-out soil, intense poverty. The story of the founding, the starting of some of these Southern mills is intensely dramatic.

Often the whole town in on it. "We may yet save our people." Memory of the cruelty of the industrial North to the agrarian South, after the Civil War—speeches, religious processions, prayers in little country towns—in Southern churches. A man from the town has gone up North, hoping to get money to build and equip a mill. Prayers going up in the little churches—"Oh, God, permit him to get it." Does it seem an exaggeration?

It's true.

The mill man talking—"How were we to get money from the Yanks if we didn't promise cheap labor, long hours? If you think I am cruel to labor, go into the back country of the South. See how cruel nature is to these men, women, and children, out on the exhausted, sun-burned hills, and plains."

In the mill towns at least isolation was broken up, education of children began. There was the modern world coming in, the movies (quarrel with them if you wish—they are often stupid enough— but at least they break poverty and isolation somewhat). Only last week I picked up, on a back road in southern Tennessee, a man and woman.

They were young Hill Billies who had been down working in a cotton-mill town and had got fired. The woman had been a leader in a strike. When the strike was over the mill wouldn't take her back. She might have been eighteen, rather pretty, but shabbily dressed, and her man might have been twenty. When I drove up they were standing by a little roadside barn in which they had slept. The woman's hair was in disorder. She carried a little package, her things, done up in a soiled handkerchief.

Lipstick. Face powder. She fixed herself after I picked them up. I could watch her through the glass stuck up at the front of the driver's seat to show the road behind.

"Ain't it a swell car?" she whispered to her man. She had come down out of the hills to work in a mill town and had got the American hunger. Earl Carroll or Florenz Ziegfeld would have taken a second look at that one. She brought a lump into my throat.

The Southern roads. You got off the big highways into little red dirt roads. Houses with dog runs. Share-croppers moving. In vacant lots in some of the poor little towns mule buying and trading going on. The share-cropper, with his family—a worn-out looking woman, plenty of kids, two or three hound dogs, a miserable few sticks of furniture on his broken-down wagon. Your thoughts—"Hell, they talk about no work in this country, not enough work. There's work here for a hundred years, giving life, modern life, to these millions."

"There is just as good stuff in these Poor Whites as in any people on earth. This idea that work for men consists only in making more cloth than people can wear, more shoes and shirts than they can wear, raising more tobacco, cotton, and corn than they can consume. How about all of us suddenly beginning to say, 'We are going to give life to people, all the possible richness of modern life'?"

"Work, that's what we Americans want, what we love. Everywhere I go people crying out, not first of all for food, clothes, comforts—but for work, work, work."

In middle Tennessee thinking of early days, old Andrew Jackson and John Sevier, fighting, swearing, horse-raising, and racing, the beautiful trotters and pacers, the Pointer family of fine horses that came up out of Tennessee—the first great westward movement in American politics, power for the first time wrested from New England and Virginia and by a middle Tennessean.

At Chattanooga—Grant, Sherman, Hood, Thomas. Sherman's forced march, with his half-frozen, battle-tired veterans, from Chattanooga to the relief of Knoxville—over this, now so well-paved highway, their feet trod.

Sherman, insane with energy, driving his men, making them love it and him. Odd that he should have been so hated in the South. Butler, yes, but not grim Sherman. He loved the Southern land—had wanted to live his life down here, among Southerners, loved the Southern sunshine, the land, the piney woods, loved the hills, and the red roads over which his men trod.

He said to the South, "You can't." It wasn't slavery that got Sherman and the Middle West into the war. He said, "An agrarian people can't, in the end, conquer an industrial people."—He

33

knew, long ago, what Lenin knew about Russia, what Japan found out.

It seems to me, now that I am again in the South, thinking South, that just now the Southern problem centres more about the poor whites of the South than about the Negro. I do not mean that life in the South hasn't also been cruel enough to the Negro. But after all, it is long-continued ignorance that, more than anything else, breeds cruelty.

These millions of Southern poor whites, tied to the poor land, long dispossessed, so often living on land that should be given back to forests, again slowly enriched in that way—you don't get the tragedy of these huge slices of America just travelling through on a train, or swiftly on paved highways in a car.

Quick glimpses—putting them aside—"Oh, they are just poor whites"—one-mule farmers or no-mule farmers—the one-gallus life—K. K. K.—lynchings——

A man must go into the little shacks, churches, lodge halls. God knows they want everything any one wants.

Is there a new realism that may help? In the South, also, even in the back country, there is talk now. You keep picking up little fragments of talk.

Government.

Government.

"Do you suppose that government—you know —the South might be made into something gorgeous. Individuals can't do it. They won't. I guess they can't."

"What is to be done is too big."

I talked to a man picked up in the road. He had been a well-to-do Southern farmer, a cotton raiser, but had lost his farm. He was a man of fifty. He said he had a daughter in Atlanta who had a stenographic job. She had asked him to come on down and live with her until he got something to do. His wife was dead. He said, "Something got started wrong between the farmers of the North and us of the South. It must have started back in slavery days," he said, "and the Civil War and what came after didn't help."

He said he had been hearing that Northern farmers had been getting it in the neck too.

"If they, up North, could be told, over and over, what we've been up against down here.

"Why should we be either Republicans or Democrats just because we happen to live down South here or up North?" he asked.

He wasn't very clear about what he had in mind, but he had been talking to others, too. He said he had been figuring a lot. He thought there should

35

be something new, bigger, taking every one in.

"I guess it'll have to be government; but it will have to be a different notion of government from what we have had," he said.

So it is in the South, too, the new feeling, the hunger. God knows what will happen when it is sold out again.

People

A Rural Realist

I PICKED up the woman on a Southern road. She might have been thirty-five. She had formerly been a cotton-mill hand and before that she was the daughter of a tenant farmer. A Southern poor white. You know how she would look—rather hard-bitten, born tired, undernourished in childhood, hook worm. There are enough of that sort.

This one didn't fit in. That's nice. It's nice that there are so many people who do not fit into the little pigeonholes our minds make for them. She didn't ask me for a ride. I saw her walking sturdily along in the road ahead and ran slowly. She looked up at me. "All right. Come on. Hop in."

She was one of the restless Americans, had come, with her father and mother, brothers, and sisters, off some tenant farm to a cotton-mill town. She was in the mill and at work at thirteen. She got married at sixteen.

She said she got tired of her husband. "He was always whining."

There had been a strike in the mill and he didn't go out with the others. He was afraid to go out and afraid not to. He sat in the house and cried.

She said it made her ashamed. On a sudden impulse, one day, she walked out of the house, in some Southern mill village, and took to the road. She said—"There are a good many of us women on the road now."

She looked at me with shrewd eyes, sizing me up.

"You ain't a gambler, are you?" she asked, I thought hopefully.

"No," I told her, "I'm a travelling man."

"Oh," she said.

She was shabbily dressed, but looked clean. We went on with our talk. "It's a rough, dirty business for a woman, isn't it, this being on the road?"

She smiled. "Do I look dirty?" Just before I picked her up, a mile back along the road, at the edge of a town, she said, she had stopped at a house and asked, "Can I come in and clean up?" There wasn't any woman in the house, only a man. "Did he try to get gay?"

"No," she said.

"Would you have left your husband if there had been children?" I asked. I took it for granted there had been none.

"No," she said.

I was curious to find out how she felt. There has been, during this depression, a growing number of these women wanderers. The wanderers, male and female, are almost a new race here in America.

"So you were a cotton-mill hand?"

"Yes, I was. I was a weaver."

There had come the strike. She went out, but her husband didn't. He got up, long before daylight, every morning and crept away unseen to the mill. She said she stayed in the house with him, for six weeks, while the strike was on, and that they didn't speak to each other. Then the strike was settled and she lit out, but first, just before the strike was settled, she went to strike headquarters about her man. She smiled grimly, telling me about that. "Do you mean you told about his sneaking into the mill to work when the strike was on, that you tipped them off?" "Yes, the bastard," she said.

They caught her husband, creeping into the mill before daylight, and beat him up.

She told me she had wandered three years.

"Do you think you will ever go back to work, settle down, perhaps get you a new man? You know what I mean—be respectable?"

"No," she said. "I don't want to now. To hell with it."

I had picked her up at the edge of one South Carolina town and let her down in another. "This is as far as I am going today," I said. She went off, down a side street.

It is odd to think of these women, pushed into a queer new kind of life by the years of depression. She was something different, formerly a cotton-mill hand, a wife. She had become an adventuress, a pure gypsy type. She had a kind of air—no beauty, but something attractive. She was a kind of rural realist, a road-hitting, hard-up Mae West, as Mae presents herself on the screen.

He Found His Racket

On the back streets of a Southern industrial town, I was waiting to go to a meeting of the unemployed, when a man panhandled me, and I gave him a dime. We walked a little way, and began to talk. We went into a little restaurant in a side street. We drank beer and talked. What struck me about him is the same thing that I have picked up everywhere. There is this curious optimism in American men. This one was an electrician. He said he hadn't got back to work yet, but was sure that he would soon.

We spoke of what he had been through. He is married to the daughter of a small farmer who lives in Ohio. When the depression hit the country his wife's father asked her to come on home, with their one child. He said, "I didn't want to go and be a load on her old man.

"I'd never been a tramp, but I became one." He was an intelligent man. "You get a new picture of life," he said.

He was curious about me. "Why are you being friendly? What are you up to? You aren't a dick, are you?"

I told him I was a writer. "Oh," he said. "You

43

are writing people up." He said he had also always wanted to be a writer.

We began talking again of his experiences. He had been to the Pacific coast. "I tried to get in as an electrician in Hollywood, but didn't make it— went to a lot of Texas cities and towns I don't even remember the names of —slept in jails."

"How does it feel?" I asked.

He told me of the curious feeling that comes to a man who has gone along for years, feeling reasonably secure. Suddenly the ground is jerked out from under his feet.

"You may stumble onto a racket." He said he did. He said he went up to a nice house, on a nice street. There was a fine-looking oldish woman who came to the door.

"I asked her, 'Could you, would you mind, giving me a few sheets of paper, an envelope, and a stamp? I've been out of work for a long time and I've been everywhere looking for work. I'd like to write a letter to my wife.' "

He said the woman took him in, gave him a meal, gave him paper, ink, and envelope, and a stamp.

"She gave me fifty cents too. It was a good racket."

"But did you write to your wife?"

"Sure I did. I been writing three or four times a day ever since.

"Now I just do a little panhandling to keep in form, but mostly just to talk to some one as we're talking. It got me woozy. I don't want to work any racket. I'm an electrician. I want to work at my job."

I had an odd experience with this man. When I was leaving him I thought, "I only gave him ten cents." I took a dollar from my pocket and held it in my hand. This was outside the little restaurant in which we had been sitting over our beer. He looked at me and at the dollar bill and grinned. "I guess writing's a racket too, eh?" he said. "Never mind, I guess maybe we'll both get back to work at our real jobs pretty soon," he said.

They Got This One

An old man, a healthy looking one, got into the car with me. He was a farmer who had lost his job. He might have been sixty-five.

An apology. They nearly all begin that way. "I've failed in this American scheme. It's my own fault." That's the tone.

"I failed. I failed. It's my own fault." You get it on all sides. There may be stupidity in it, but there is also humility. It gives you occasionally at night a dream of what we Americans, properly led by men who can be at least partially disinterested, may some day do.

The job?

"Where's the job? Lead me to it."

The breaking down of the moral fiber of the American man, through being out of a job, losing that sense of being some part of the moving world of activity, so essential to an American man's sense of his manhood—the loss of this essential something in the jobless can never be measured in dollars.

This one wasn't quite broke. He was neatly dressed, in a worn gray suit, such a suit as a fairly well-to-do farmer would have for his Sunday best. The suit would have been bought years before. It had got thin, was mended here and there. He had the big-knuckled hands of the man who has worked all of his life out of doors in the fields.

The talk between us began slowly. I tried being frank with him. "I'm a writer, scouting about. I try to pick up little stories of people and write them down for a magazine. I want to find out how the depression has affected people, what kind of outlook they feel they have for the future." The idea interested him as it does most people.

He was just a farmer without much education, he said. He had a daughter. There had been two children, a son and a daughter, but he lost his son in the World War. His farm, one hundred and twenty acres, was in southern Indiana. He said that he and his wife had led pretty hard lives, trying to educate both the children, send them off to college. Both the children had taken to book learning. His son left college to go to the war.

All of this came out slowly. The man was with me most of two days. In the town where we stayed overnight I urged him to come to my hotel. "Come on. Be my guest. You know, just this once."

"No," he said firmly. He thought he could find

47

a bed, maybe for a quarter. "You ought to have seen the bed me and my wife slept on when we were first married. We went into debt for our farm. It was before we got the farm paid for and built the new house and fixed it up."

He had lost his farm by going into debt. It was during the World War, when prices for farm products were high and land high. His son wasn't going to be a farmer. He wanted to be a doctor, and his daughter also was the book-learning sort. "I don't know why they turned out to be that way, but they did and me and my wife were proud of them." After the war and the death of the son, his daughter married a man she met in school. He was a young, poorly-paid professor of modern languages in a small Southern college, and my farming man had wanted to set them up in a house of their own, all paid for. "I liked her man all right, but knew he'd never make any money. I didn't put a plaster on their house. I put it on my land and went in debt for some more land."

So that was his story. They had closed in on him and his wife got sick and died. He was going South to live with his daughter and her husband. "If I had been younger, the bank might have let me stay on my land, but they got a younger man who wanted it."

48

His face worked. It isn't nice to see such a man shot to pieces. I began talking quickly of other things. He had never seen his daughter's place. He wondered if there was much ground.

The place was right in a town. If there was enough ground to have a good garden, it might be all right. When he was on his own place, he never fooled with the garden. His wife did that, but he thought he could put his hand to it. He did hope it was good ground.

"If a man feels he is being useful, making something grow, to feed people—" He knew that in some southern Indiana towns, the bigger ones, you couldn't keep a cow or a pig. The hardest part about leaving his own place was leaving his team. "I always had the best team for miles around," he said.

Mound Diggers

THE archæologists, Doctor Coburn and Doctor Jennings, were not wanderers. They were digging out a mound-builders' mound, on the shore of a little river in a valley between high mountains.

I thought they had found something significant just now. What interested me most was what they found above, not below, the ground. I saw a hundred men working in an open field, and turned in. It was one of the smaller CWA projects. The mound was in a flat field that had been planted last year to corn.

The mound was being opened very carefully and scientifically, in the interest of the Smithsonian in Washington, and these two archæologists had been lent, one I was told by the University of Michigan, the other by the University of Chicago. They were absorbed, happy men.

What interested me, got me fascinated, was the workmen, and what the two archæologists had found out about workmen. The workers on the job were hill billies, many of them supposedly stupid, illiterate men.

The two college men had not found them stupid. They had tapped something in the workers. This in a country of old feuds, of makers of moon liquor, of lynchings. How many men have told me, "You can do little or nothing with such people. They are poor whites, almost a distinct race. They are impossible." Doctor Coburn came up to where I stood on a mound of discarded earth.

The land on which the mound stood had been given to the government by the owner, a fairly well-to-do farmer, without cost—only——

"You must give the work to my neighbors, on the hills around here."

The thought of what it must have meant to the workmen, at the beginning, the foolishness of it all. "Well, if the government wants to do it—it's the government's funeral."

"This silly business, authentic factual history of an ancient people. What t'll? Give me a bottle of moon. That's authentic and factual enough for me."

But there had been something tapped, something old and pretty first-rate in man. The workmen on the job had quickly come alive with interest. Leaders had sprung out from among them,

51

I dare say there had been, at first, patient explanation of the purpose of what was being done. I know there had been. I went at night to a country school house with the two college men, heard their patient explanation to men, women, and children. They told me how they had gone for many such nights to many country school houses, into homes in the hills, calling meetings of the people and explaining.

And the workmen, these hill billies, had caught on. There was an intense absorption. How swift, how light-fingered they had become. Two or three foremen, also mountain hill billies, walked about. "We could almost go away and leave the work to them now." Eagerness. "Here is something unearthed. Handle it carefully. It may crumble away under your fingers. It has been in here, who knows how long, it may be a thousand years."

Old records of ancient men's lives. That didn't absorb me. When the work was done for the day, I followed a hill billie across a field toward a shed where tools were put away. "Did you find anything today?"

"No, sir, but I bet you I git something tomorrow." He was like the rest of the workmen on the job, alive with interest. I thought of what so many people have told me about this CWA work, the work of the boys in the CCC camps. "It won't amount to a thing," many people keep saying. "If a man really wants work, he'll find it for himself. If a man is out of work, it is because he's no good."

There is plenty to be learned yet.

The TVA

THERE is the Tennessee River. It starts up in the Blue Ridge country. Little rivers come racing down, the Clinch, the Holston, and others. The Tennessee is a hill-country river, working its way down valleys, under big hills, little hills, now creeping west, now south, now north —Virginia, West Virginia, Kentucky, Tennessee, down into northern Alabama. The hill country of north Georgia is in the TVA sphere of influence. That is what this TVA thing is, "a sphere of influence."

It is something to dream and hope for, this land drained by the Tennessee. There are a few rich valleys, growing blue grass. There are mountain ranges. Once all these mountains and hills were covered with magnificent forests. It was one of the two Morgans who are in charge of this vast enterprise with David Lilienthal, H. A. Morgan, the land man, the folk man of the project, who talked to me of that. He was president of the University of Tennessee before he got into this thing and he is a land-man.

He talked for an hour and I got a sharp sense

of the land-loving man. There was the story of how the hill lands had been robbed. No use blaming any one. The big timber men came to denude the hills. Then the little ones with the "peckerwood" mills came to clean up.

The farmers were left on the hills. Traditions grew up about these people. John Fox wrote of them in *The Trail of the Lonesome Pine*. Not so good. Jeeter, of Erskine Caldwell's *Tobacco Road*, is nearer the real thing. They were of the feud country, a pretty romantic lot, in books and stories. In real life they were something else—in real life it was a pitiful rather than a romantic story.

It was the story of a people clinging, year after year, to little hillside farms. Every year they got poorer and poorer. Some of these men went out of their hills to the coal mines and later to the factory towns that had come into the hills, but many came back. There is the love of his own country in the hill man. He does not want to leave the hills.

The depression brought the hill men back faster. I went into little upland valleys where a farm of thirty or forty acres might once have sustained one family. (It would have been poor enough fare—hard enough living for the one family.)

But now, often, on such a farm I found three or four families. Sons had come back to their mountain fathers, bringing wives, bringing children. They had built little huts—often without windows.

"At least here, on my father's land, a little corn can be raised. There will be a cabin floor to sleep on at night. It is less terrible than walking among the out-of-works, in some industrial town."

There is a story of an Englishman coming into the hill country, going among the hill men. The Englishman was stunned.

"These hill men are English," he said. "I don't like it."

"You don't like what?"

"I don't like their failing; I don't like to think of Englishmen as failures in a new land."

It is a land of tall, straight men—the kind of stock out of which came Daniel Boone, Andrew Jackson, Andrew Johnson. They have fine looking children, these men. The children fade young. The women fade young.

There is bad diet. No money. The soil gets thinner and thinner with every passing year. Most of this hill land should go back into forest. Every rain that washes down the hillsides takes more of the soil away.

Suppose you put the hills back into forest, what are you to do with these people? Are you to herd them down into industrial cities, where there are already too many men out of work, living on charity?

You have to think of the fact that what we call the modern world has pretty much gone on past these people, as it has gone completely past the tenant farmers, farther South. There are these mountaineers, millions of them scattered over a vast territory, touching several states. These are not the foreigners of whom we Americans can say so glibly—"If they do not like it here, let them go back where they came from." These men are from the oldest American stock we have. It is the kind of stock out of which came Abraham Lincoln. Robert Lincoln, his father, and Nancy Hanks, his mother, were poor whites of the hills.

And there is all this other stuff about us of which we Americans are so proud, our well-equipped houses, motor cars, bathrooms, warm clothes— what we call our American standard of living. All these things not touching these mountain people.

They are clinging to their hills in one of the most beautiful lands in the world.

"Can we take what they and their hills already have—adding nothing—find the riches in their hills—and give these men modern life? If this modern mechanical life is any good, it should be good for these people."

There is wealth in the land on which these people have tried to live. It is a new kind of wealth, the wealth of the modern man, of the modern world. It is wealth in the form of energy.

Power—the coinage of the modern world!

There is plenty of power—the private companies have only got a little of it so far—flowing silently away, along the, Tennessee, along the rivers that come down out of the hills to make the Tennessee.

Long ago, I'm told, army engineers went through these hills. They drew up a kind of plan, having in mind the use of all this wasted power in case of war, power to be harnessed, to make munitions, to kill men.

There came the World War and the building of the Wilson Dam at Muscle Shoals. That is where the Tennessee, in its wanderings, dips down into northern Alabama, thrusts down into the land of cotton. It is something to be seen. All good Americans should go and see it. If the Russians had it there would be parades, special editions of illustrated magazines got out and distributed by the government.

There it is, however, completely magnificent. You go down, by elevator, some ten stories, under the earth, under the roaring river, and walk out into great light clean rooms. There is a song, the song of the great motors. You are stirred. Something in you—the mechanically-minded American in you, begins to sing. Everything is so huge, so suggestive of power and at the same time so delicate. You walk about muttering.

"No wonder the Russians wanted our engineers," you say to yourself.

The great motors sing on, each motor as large as a city room. There is a proud kind of rebirth of Americanism in you.

"Some of our boys did this," you say to yourself, throwing out your chest.

The Wilson Dam never was made to impound much water. The idea was to take the power directly out of the swirl of water rushing down over the shoals.

But sometimes it doesn't rush. Dry seasons come, far up-river and in the little rivers. The forest-denuded hills do not hold back the water after rains. Every time you build another dam up-river you get power out of the new dam and you increase the power at Muscles Shoals. They are building two dams now, each to make a great lake, the Joe Wheeler, some twenty-five miles above the Wilson, and the Norris, far up-river, a day's drive, near Knoxville. They will both make great lakes, the shore line of the Norris to be some nine hundred miles, it to be at places two hundred feet deep.

Power stored to make a steady stream of power —power from the Wilson being used to build the Joe Wheeler and the Norris—the river being made to harness itself. There is a new kind of poetry in that thought.

These, the first of perhaps a dozen dams to be built along one river—power aplenty for great stretches of country far outside the sphere of influence of the present TVA.

The power to be used, to give an opportunity to small industries, reduce the power costs in towns over a wide country, make electrical power available in homes where it cannot now be used—the money coming in to go back into the country out of which the power came——

Denuded hills to be reforested, soil washing stopped.

This soil washing, going on in every denuded hill country, filling your lakes with mud after you build your dams, utterly destroying, making a barren waste of wide stretches of country. It's hard to dramatize the slow, steady year-after-year eating away of soil richness. Whole lands have been destroyed by it, made into deserts. The government foresters, working with the CCC boys, are like wronged children in their eagerness to make their work understood. "Tell them about it. Please tell them," they keep saying. They follow you around eagerly. "You are a writer. Can't you tell them? Can't you make them understand that we are builders? These CCC camps. We are taking these city kids and making builders of them. The boys in the camps begin to understand. Please make every one understand."

Engineers and foresters going at night, after the day's work, to country towns in the district, to country school houses, lecturing, explaining. I found in these men working on the TVA something I have been hungry to find, men working at work they love, not thinking of money or promotion, happy men, laughing men. They think they are saving something. They think they are making something.

I went into the TVA accompanied by a friend, a business man who lives in Chicago. Formerly he was a college professor. Once he wrote a beautiful novel that got little or no attention. He was poor and went into business. He succeeded.

But like a good many American business men,

he wasn't very happy in his success. When the New Deal was announced he went in for it, head over heels.

He was strong for the NRA, but recently he has been skeptical. I had written him, telling him that I was going to look at the TVA and he wanted to go along. We met in Knoxville and spent most of the first night in a hotel room, talking.

He was discouraged.

"It isn't going to work," he said. He was speaking of the NRA. "They are trying to fix prices now. The small man is doomed." He is himself not one of the small men. "You can't stop the chisellers. You can't. You can't."

We went to look at the TVA. We did look. We listened. We went down among the workers on the dams. We went into power houses, visited men in their offices. Sometimes we were accompanied by enthusiasts, engineers, foresters, and others, and often we were alone. We had our own car.

We kept talking. We kept looking. A change came over my friend.

"So this is the South," he said.

He had the Northern man's point of view. To the Southerner the South is the deep South. He began talking of the TVA as the South's opportunity. In spite of the fact that my friend was once a college professor he is an educated man. He knows his American history.

"Look what we Northerners did to the South," he kept saying as his enthusiasm grew. "And now this."

We took our look at the TVA, the immediate sphere of influence, and pushed on down into the deep South. We got into the back country, going by back roads.

Men were plowing in the Southern fields. There was the thing, always a new wonder to the city man, the patience of men with the earth, the way they cling to it. We were in a poor district. They are not hard to find in the back country of the deep South. There were these miles of back roads, deeply rutted, even dangerous, bridges fallen into decay.

"It is a kind of inferno," my friend kept saying. We had just left the land of new hope, men busy, the strikingly charming government-built town of Norris, at Norris Dam, going up, men laughing at their work——

Memory in us both of a lunch had with a dozen foresters in a town in the heart of the TVA—the town sitting on land that would presently be a lake bottom—the laughter in the room, the anxiety of the men that their story be told straight——

63

"Don't talk too big. Don't promise too much. We may be stopped."

That against the land of desolation, of no hope —the poor farmers, getting poorer every year. The cotton allotment in the South wasn't going to be of much help to the people along the road we had got into. It would go to the land owners and not one out of ten of the little farmers, white or black, along the road we travelled would own the land he was plowing——

Poor little unpainted cabins half fallen down. Pale women with tired eyes. Undernourished children playing in bare yards before the cabins.

"There are too many of these."

We had got into an argument. My friend had lived his boyhood on an Iowa farm.

"You have places as bad as this in your Chicago," I said, not wanting him to think all American misery was in the South.

"I know, but not on the land! In the end, everything comes back to the land."

"The people who cannot love the land on which they live are a lost people."

"It is right that all America should try this experiment in the South," he said. There were the one-mule farmers patiently plowing the land beside the road.

"It is wonderful the way man goes on. In spite of defeat he goes on," my friend said.

Two old men came out of a strip of pine woods. They were toothless, bent old men, Southerners, poor whites, going along the road in silence. We passed them.

My friend leaned out of the car. He was excited.

"Hey!" he called.

The two old men stopped and stared at us. I stopped the car. My friend hesitated.

"Drive on," he said. He turned to me and laughed. "I wanted to tell them something. I can't," he said. "It would sound too silly."

"What?" I said.

"Something new in American life is begun back there, and it mustn't be stopped," he said. I thought it was the feeling, alive in him, as it is still curiously alive in so many Americans, alive in spite of greed, chiseling, desire for fake money, bigness. The feeling of men for men—desire to some day work for others. The TVA may be a beginning.

Tough Babes in the Woods

Tough Babes in the Woods

THEY have made a little town under the hill
—between two hills—in a narrow valley
down which flows a mountain stream. This
in one of a dozen such little towns I have been in
during the last week, and they are all pretty much
alike. There is an army man and a forester or two
in each camp. The army men have charge of the
camp. They differ. Some add little home-like
touches, others do not. There may be twenty or
thirty or fifty houses in such a camp town, and it
may have one street or two or three. They are
laying down sidewalks in the one I have just been
in. This is the time of mud in the valleys and in
the hills. Soon the spring rains will be coming
here.

The boys in this camp town, at the edge of which
I am sitting—I am sitting with my notebook on a
flat stone under a rhododendron bush—the boys
go up the hills and bring down flat stones. They
are laying sidewalks along the street down which
I look, making their town neat against the muddy
time to come. A man goes about among them
directing the work, a tall lean intelligent man of

thirty. He is the forester of this camp—a soft-speaking Southerner—and this is Saturday, so the boys do not go to work in the woods. It is a clear quiet day and rather warm. Spring will be coming soon in this Southern Appalachian country. I hear a little animal moving back of me in the woods. A hawk floats in the clear blue sky above the valley.

When I drove over to this mountain camp this morning I saw a man plowing a hillside above the next valley to the South. He was a lean, ragged, hard-bitten mountain man, and he lived in a one-room cabin at the end of the field he was plowing. I have seen as many as nineteen children in one family in such a cabin. I have seen poverty that has made me halt. I have seen a thousand such cabins perched on hills in southwestern Virginia, Pennsylvania, West Virginia, Tennessee, north Georgia, Kentucky, and westward, across the Mississippi, in the Ozark mountains of the Missouri, and only two weeks ago, in the city of New York, I saw just such a cabin on the stage, in a play called *Tobacco Road.*

Tobacco Road, indeed! It is a road to ruin—this Poor White hillside farming going on year after year, over millions of acres of the American hill country. As for the Poor White Georgia

Cracker man of the Georgia plains, tied to his cotton and tobacco farming on poor exhausted soil, his story is a different one. We are in the hills now. This is the story of the hill man. The story here also one of wasted fine material. I know the mountain men, and when I am at home I live among them. The story of the lives they live, how they got like that, the death of the children of this fine stock by undernourishment—this is another tragic American story. How I have hated the romanticists who have thrown the cloud of romance about such lives.

But I am trying to tell now the story of the camp towns, of the CCC coming to these hills. They are scattered out over the country, hundreds, even thousands of such little temporary towns—the government putting them up. The houses of the towns are long one-story affairs built of thick building paper. They stand up high and dry above the valley bottoms on stone foundations.

There is a commissary building, a mess hall, a post office, a library, a temporary hospital. They are all temporary houses.

Suppose they shouldn't be temporary. Suppose what is going on here is but a beginning. It is an interesting idea that this thing that has now begun in America—government having a thought of the land, men in Washington, in government, daring to say—"We'll begin trying it."

Trying what?

Suppose it should come down to this, that there is a plot on foot in America—men actually serious about it—a plot, let's say, to save America from the Americans.

Actually they are serious about the plot, some of them. I have been in Washington—talked to men there, men who struck me as first-rate, serious-minded men—not at all romantic. I do not mean bankers or industrialists. I mean men of another type—scientific men, government engineers, foresters, hard-working men, most of whom have been employed for years in the Interior and the Agricultural departments.

Much of what these men told me is, as they say in Washington now—"off the record." It is still, it seems, somewhat irregular even a little dangerous to have dreams of a greater America, an America really used. You can't call names.

"What, you dream of a physical America controlled, plowing of the land controlled—this or that section of America to be permanently in forest —river flow control, floods controlled at the flood source?"

"You say that one great flood—let us say of

Mother Mississippi—may cost more than ten years' constructive work back in the hills, in denuded forests where floods begin?"

"This, off the record. Some one may think I am a Socialist or a Bolshevik."

Men's minds pushing, somewhat timidly, into a new social view of physical America. How are they to tell the story to that lean mountain man? Let us say that he owns his few poor hillside acres. Who is to tell him, "Thou shalt not"? The right to go on plowing, where plowing is sheer land destruction—the traditional right of the American individualist, big or little.

"It's mine."

"It's mine."

Who is to say to me, a free American, "Thou shalt not"?

Into this camp have come boys, the greater number of them from American cities. They are young boys, most of them about high school age. But for this depression, in the natural flow of an older American life—it seems suddenly old now—as things have been running in America for the last two, three or four generations these boys, being for the most part city and town boys, would have come out of school and would have become clerks or factory hands.

Or—and this would go for a lot of them—they would have become tough city guys—the kind that make bright young gangsters—the kind you see leaning against walls near gang hangouts in cities.

"How much to kill a man?"

"How much?"

But, you see, even the rackets have become a bit thin now, clerkships have fallen away, prohibition has gone, the factories are not exactly howling for men.

So these CCC camps have gathered them in, all kinds of men.

That forester down there, directing the boys as they lay sidewalks in their new woods town, was in Montana last year. He had under him out there some two or three hundred boys, mostly from the East Side of New York—tough birds—most of them, he says. He speaks of them with an affectionate grin. "Boy, what we had to do to them—what they did to us." They have been jerked up out of that environment, hauled in fast trains across two-thirds of the United States and thrown into a forest camp some seven thousand feet up in the magnificent hills. They had to build the camps, keep themselves clean, keep their bedding and their quarters clean, learn to swing an axe— "We had to watch them like babes that they did not kill each other with the axes." The boys learned to make beds, learned the necessary sanitary laws that must govern men living in camps, the give and take of man to man, so essential to life where men live, sleep, talk, dream in one great room—rows of cots all in the open—the door at the end of the room open—sight of the wooded hills when you go to sleep at night, when you wake in the morning——

These men, the greater majority of them out of the crowded factory towns.

"It's the beginning of some kind of revolution in life—for them at least."

"Sure."

Not every man can swing an axe. Some men born in the forests, never get the knack. There are Babe Ruths among axemen too.

It is a kind of revolution in many lives that goes both backward and forward. Forward, let's say, to a possible conception of an America that shall belong essentially to all Americans—as one thoughtful, serious-minded man, who felt he owed something to the ground under his feet, might feel toward one farm—such a man as might say to himself—"I want to leave this piece of ground, on which I have lived my life and made my living, a better piece of ground than it was when I came upon it." You get the idea—at least a dream of all American farmers saying "We'll live to build, not destroy."

Something of that sort.

Let's say, a new comprehensive forward look and then also, in this CCC thing something else —a kind of movement backward to an earlier American tone of life, when life did centre about the forests and the land, when men went out and fought it out with nature and got something men can get in no other way—a kind of man-making process that factory work and clerkships haven't as yet been able to bring into men's lives.

To use the land also to make men.

To use men also to make the land.

Who in America doesn't know what, over great stretches of country, we Americans have done to the land? Soil erosion going on that is costing us each year more than the entire cost of our military and naval establishments, and all of this due to the old belief that if I own a piece of land I have the right to do as I please with it. I can tear off the forest.

"It's mine, isn't it?"

The valley down which I look as I sit writing is one of a thousand such valleys in the range of mountains that stretch across our country from East to West, separating the North from the South. It is a stream-source country. This country with the great stretches of cut-over lands in northern Michigan, Wisconsin, and Minnesota is the stream source from which comes much of the water of the Mississippi. The valley down which I look is watered by one of the little rivers that come down from the hills. There might be fifty such streams in one county in this country. The natives tell me that all were formerly good trout and bass streams. They went softly along through the deep woods. They were icy cold even in summer. They were steady year-round streams, fed by mountain springs. The valley is broken by many little side valleys. It is like an old saw with many teeth broken out. In each little side valley may be found a few under-fed mountain families, persistently plowing hillside lands that will not and cannot make them a living.

These CCC camps are a beginning. If you look at the map you will see them scattered most thickly along the Pacific Coast, north at the headwaters of the Mississippi and in these border mountains between the North and South, and on the southern side of these hills where the streams go down to the Atlantic. There are camps now everywhere in these hills along the Southern Appalachian, the Cumberland, the Blue Ridge, and westward to the Mississippi and the Ozarks. They extend eastward to where, at Lynchburg, Virginia, the big hills end and the little ones step softly down to the Tide-water country.

It may well be that all of this land, except only the valley bottoms, should be wiped out as farming lands. Let the trees again have the hills. There should be better use for the life of these hill men, starving and destroying in these hills.

The hand of government is reaching out and out. The government is acquiring all the time more and more thousands of acres of these hill lands.

They are having classes in the camps. They are teaching geography and history. As the boys work in the forests, a forester goes with them. They are learning to tell the ash from the maple and the spruce from the oak. It is a tremendous educational experiment.

The greater number of the boys are city bred. They are from the families of the poor. They are young American born—Poles, Italians, Jews, Lithuanians, and Germans—the first generation away from the old country. They are short squat figures of American men in the making, with the twang of the city speech on their lips. Nearly all of the boys in this camp town are out of the back streets of Newark, Hoboken, Jersey City, and New York. "Where are you from, buddy?" I say to one of them.

"Oh, take a look. What do you t'ink?"

"I'm from Avenue A."

The mountain men who come into the camp, to work, or just to look, stand staring at the city boys. They laugh softly. Such awkward axe-swinging. Some of these mountain men have been axe-swingers since they were babes. Some of them, the older ones, worked in the lumber camps in these hills when the first forests, the great forests, were cut away. They tell you about it. First the great companies with the big band mills came, taking the best, and these were followed by the little pecker-wood mills—often a model T Ford engine and a saw, cleaning up what the big ones left.

There was destruction and waste aplenty. Who cared? Individualism. The old America. "You should have seen it before they came," an old mountain man said. A kind of awe creeps into his voice. "The forest was like a great church. Oh, the great trees. You sank to your knees in the moss under foot."

I myself remember an old man who came to my father's house when I was a boy. He was an old,

old man from an Ohio River town where my own father once lived and he talked to my father of the river. "I remember when I was a boy," he said. "I swam with other boys in the Ohio. It was a clear stream then. We used to swim way out and look down. The water was so clear we could see the bottom."

There is something still to be seen in this CCC movement. It isn't just an idea of giving a certain number of men work, helping them over the depression.

The leaves of the forest trees, even the young new trees, now growing, fall and lie on the ground. Next year more leaves fall. There is a soft porous bottom made. Moss begins to grow. It is a great blotter. Pinchot of Pennsylvania, when he was making his first fight against forest destruction, used to go before control committees with a wide board in his hand. He set the board on a table at an angle of forty-five degrees and poured a glass of water down it.

Then he took the same board and tacked blotting paper on it. Again he poured water down the board, but this time it did not rush off. That told the story. It is a thing the government can do and that the individual cannot do. There are these millions of acres of water-shed land, none of it any good for farming. It should go back into forests, making future wealth.

Rains come and wash the plowed lands away and every rain takes its toll of richness. You go through these hill lands in the spring and summer, seeing the hill men at the plow, often on lands so steep you wonder that the man and bony horse do not both roll to the bottom—men slowly and painfully plowing, planting, and hoeing—then the rains— there the fields go.

It would not have mattered so much if it were only one field, a few fields plowed and lost, great gashes in the hillsides, water rushing down pell-mell, floods in the low lands, towns destroyed. There are still millions of such fields being plowed. The whole country pays.

Multiply it. Multiply it.

The forester comes up to me along the street of the camp. He sees me sitting and writing under the rhododendron bush and hesitates. "Hello," I say.

"I do not want to disturb you."

We grin at each other. "Come on," he says.

Putting my notebook into my pocket I go and get into his truck and we begin climbing up a mountain road. It's risky going. This is one of the new roads the city boys have made. It rained last night and the car slithers about. Up and up we go, far up into the hills and the car stops. We go on afoot. We go into the brush. Climbing over fallen logs, up and up. "I wanted to show you a tree they didn't get," he says, referring to the early lumber men. We stop before a great spruce far up in the hills. "They had to leave it," he says. "They couldn't get to it."

We are sitting now on a rocky promontory and looking way over the hills. From up here the smaller hills are like the waves of the sea in a storm. The man I am with is one of the believers. He talks and talks. He is sore at the lumberman who beat him into these forests.

"The government should never have let them do it," he keeps saying. "We should have had a chance. Our men should have been here." He declares that under the foresters the lumber companies might have taken as much lumber without denuding the hills. "They could have taken out all the good timber and left the half-grown trees that in another generation would have made a second great cutting."

Now it will take us fifty years to get back what was wantonly destroyed. He stands beside me on the mountain top swearing, but it is already an old story to me, this cry of the forester. Now they are in the woods again. They are directing the work of these boys in the CCC camps.

The depression has given them their chance. "Hurrah for the depression," one of them said to me. They are making a new kind of American man out of the city boy in the woods, and they are planning at least to begin to make a new land with the help of such boys.

Blue Smoke

Blue Smoke

You begin with the ground—Ground lugs —Bright lugs—Yellow red—Long red— Short red and tips.

The big tobacco warehouse and sales-room is at the edge of a town over the Virginia line in Tennessee. There are these big tobacco warehouses and sales-rooms in a dozen towns within a morning's truck-driving distance of the town from which I write, and there are tobacco farmers in town from over in Virginia, from North Carolina, from Kentucky, and even from South Carolina.

A learned man at the post office in one of these towns told me that this Southern Appalachian country is one of the oldest in the world. He says he got it out of a book. He says that is the reason why the hills are so soft and round. The towns are tucked away in the valleys in the hills. From the hilltops there are little white towns with many church spires.

A man from within ten miles of this town may take his tobacco to a Virginia or South Carolina town, and a man from far over in Kentucky may try his luck here. The towns scream on billboards along the highways. The towns shout, "TAKE

YOUR TOBACCO TO GREENVILLE."
"TRY ABINGDON." "ASHEVILLE, THE
BEST TOBACCO MARKET IN THE
SOUTH."

The towns want the market. The merchants hunger for it. In Asheville, two years ago, a merchant explained to me. That year the banks began cracking up down there. "If we hadn't got a pretty good tobacco market we'd have been done for," he said. The market may be important to the merchant, eager for the farmer's money, but it's ten times as important to the little tobacco raisers. They come into town filled with what the economists call "income expectancy."

What happens to them here, at this market, is the turning point of the year.

To many of them it means a year's income, all they will get. The kids need shoes and maybe a new suit or dress. And there is the "old woman," the tobacco farmer's wife. Just because she is called the "old woman" doesn't mean she is old. She is usually long and lean as is her "old man." This is still the hill country, little farms tucked away in little valleys in the hills—"hollers," they call them.

"Where's your place, Luther?"

I am not going to try to write in the dialect of the country.

"Why, I'm a Scott County man. It's in Scratch-gravel Holler." He's a Virginian, that one. He has come over here into Tennessee, to try his luck in this Tennessee market. The native Virginian never locates himself by a town. He doesn't say, "I'm from over near Lynchburg, or Charlottes-ville," as a Middle-Western man would. He says, "I'm from Grayson, or Scott, or Albemarle," naming his county. I remember a Virginia Floyd County woman who had married into Augusta County. "How are you, Mrs. Greer?" I asked. "I'm just common," she said, "except I'm honing for Floyd." It's good. It's a land, not a town at-tachment.

The men stand wistfully in the road before the tobacco market. Some of them have come to the market alone, others have brought their families. The tobacco farmer rarely has a truck of his own to bring his tobacco to market. "I'm too small a feller for that," he explains. He may own a Model T Ford. You can't haul much tobacco in that.

So he goes in with half a dozen neighbors and they hire a truck to do the hauling—John's tobacco, Jim's, Luther's, Fred's. "A little feller like I am can't put out much, maybe one acre, or two, or three."

"It's really a woman's crop," John says.

"You've got to mess and mess with it, all year long." He stands before the warehouse, where the selling is going on. Luther and Jim and Fred stand with him. Fred has had a few shots of moon. You can smell it on him. He keeps slapping Jim on the back and laughing, rather foolishly. He says two of his kids, little fellers, put out half an acre for themselves. He helped them. They are both boys, and one of them wants a bicycle and the other some red-top boots. A man named Love comes up. "Hello, Love," Fred says, and I am a bit startled. "Is that really your name?" I want to ask. Love is built like another Abraham Lincoln. He has a long, scrawny neck, and there are bright red spots on his cheeks. "Look out or tuberculosis will get you," I think. He stands and spits on the ground. He is suspicious of me.

"You ain't a government man, are you?"

Formerly, in these hills, among these hill men, to admit you were a government man, that you had anything to do with government—to say the least, it was somewhat dangerous.

But times have changed. They have changed fast in the last year. There is a curious, wistful looking toward government now. Government becomes, to these little men, grubbing in the earth in these little valleys, curiously the Almost God.

Personified in Mr. Roosevelt. They are nice about it, but it has its connotations. These little farmers have been stripped naked by the money-changers time and again. I suspect that these men could be made into brown or black or silver shirts easily enough. They hunger for leadership, and are looking to government and to Franklin D. Roosevelt with a curious boyish faith. "We can't do it by ourselves," they keep saying. They feel dimly that the big tobacco and cigarette companies are the common enemy. "We can't handle 'em. Government's got to help us or we're lost." Government at Washington is something far away and outside local county and state government, "the law."

"Look out. Here comes the law." A short fat man, a deputy sheriff, walks past us.

The men keep speaking of Roosevelt. "Ain't going to blame him for nothing he can't do." As though to say—"don't expect too much." There is this curious sweetness, humility, in these common men. A man going about among them, as I am doing just now, keeps asking himself, "Why does any one want to cheat them or hurt them?"

Most of the tobacco in this country is raised in small patches, one or two or three or at the most five acres. It is Burley tobacco. It's an exacting crop. You work at it all through the year. Now

91

the tobacco is going to market and the farmer who has just sold his crop will go home from here to burn over his seed bed for next year's crop.

For the seed bed he'll try to find a little patch of new rich ground, usually at the edge of the woods. The ground for the seed bed needs to be rich, so he selects the new ground, and if it isn't rich enough, he piles on the manure or the fertilizer.

Then he burns it over, puts on some dry litter and burns it off. The seed goes in and he takes a trip to town and buys strips of cheese-cloth to spread over the patch. Soon now you will see the little white patches over these hills.

Hoeing and cultivating and working all through the year. In the spring the fields blossom with a mass of lovely white bloom, a sight to see. You leave a few blossoms for next year's seed plants, but all the rest of the blossoms you take off. Fred says he nips his out with his fingers, but Luther says he uses a knife.

Then there is the harvest. It's a ticklish matter getting this crop in. When it comes to the sales warehouse, the sale floor, everything counts for you or against you. What you want, to get the price, is the great wide thin bright yellow tobacco leaves. Leaves can be so easily spotted and spoiled.

They can dry too fast or too slow. If they are seasoned just right they will be soft, like soft silk.

But to get them that way is a job. It takes the skill and the know-how. As I have already said, it begins at the ground. You break off the lower leaves, bind them together into a "hand." That's your "ground lugs." You won't get so much for your ground lugs. The rains have washed up onto the leaves. They are discolored where they have touched the ground. They will be coarse and spotty. Then come your "bright lugs," your "yellow red," your "long red." Here's your money tobacco, if it's cured right. Your "tips," at the very top of the plant are likely to be small, broken and spotty. They will go off at a low price. They will make snuff or cheap smoking tobacco.

When you have cut your tobacco you build racks in the field and let it hang out to dry. That is to get your fine yellow color.

Then into the barn. You want a barn the rain can't get into but that lets in plenty of air.

Now comes the grading, time to have an eye in your head, to have feel in your fingers. Fred says, "Can't one man in ten grade tobacco. It's like picking a new dress for a woman."

Now the tobacco goes into the sales warehouse.

93

It is carefully piled, each grade in a separate basket, and now come the buyers, the auctioneer and the pin hookers.

The pin hookers are a special breed. Some of them do nothing else but this all through the year. They work two months and rest ten. The big rush in the tobacco market lasts through January and February. The pin hooker is a man who knows his tobacco. He lives and bets on his knowledge. He is a man often who never raised a stalk of tobacco in his life, but he is a trader, and a sharp one. He knows his tobacco, and he knows his Fred, his Luther, Jim, and Tom. Life is a poker game for him.

The tobacco market is a kind of fair. Every one comes. The great, roomy warehouse is out at the edge of town near the railroad.

The patent medicine man has come, and the horse trader is here. There are long lines of trucks waiting for their turn to get tobacco on to the floor. The warehouse is owned by a private company. It takes off a percentage for every pound of tobacco sold. When there is a big market a farmer may be two or three days getting his crop on to the sales floor. He has brought a basket of food from home, and often at night he and the old woman and the kids sleep on the tobacco in the truck.

Then, during the daytime you walk about and watch the sale. Hope. Hope. Hope. There are only four or five big tobacco companies in America, and each has its buyer here. The buyers are young, shrewd, fast-thinking, clever.

The men go to the sales floor and come back. The tobacco is stacked in long rows. Now they are selling Tom Whistler's baskets. How indifferent the buyers appear! Can they know what this means to Tom? You have been in a hospital and have seen a surgeon cut a man's arm off. It's like that. Each buyer puts his arm into the basket and jerks out a hand of the tobacco. He holds it up to the light, feels the leaves, throws the hand back into the basket.

"Eight-fifty."

"Nine."

That is Tom Whistler standing over there with his wife and kids. This sale is to decide everything for him. This is his year's income. Will the wife get a new dress, the kids new shoes? Will he have money to pay his taxes? I saw a tall man sitting on top of his basket after the buyers had passed. He put his face down in his hands and cried. Love pointed him out to me.

"Fred got four cents for his crop last year," Love says to me. "Did Fred cry? No! Fred went out and got a bottle of moon and that night he got pie-eyed."

The tobacco industry is a big, regulated, controlled industry. But the little farmers feel it isn't controlled for them. Some of them talk about it as they stand in the warehouse and in the street, waiting.

The pin hooker moves about among them. He goes to a farmer whose crop has not yet been sold. He tempts the farmer. Some few of the farmers, the smart ones, those who know how to cure and grade their tobacco, know as much as the pin hooker. Others are unfortunate. "A lot of us are pretty dumb," Fred says. The pin hooker makes a flat offer. If he sees a basket he thinks is badly graded, he will go to the farmer, buy it and regrade it. There are the pin hookers who work outside and the floor pin hookers. I stood on the floor on a day when tobacco took a sharp jump upward. A pin hooker wearing a fancy vest and with a big cigar in his mouth came and spoke to me. "I shaved off eight hundred bucks today," he said. By a little sharp trading he had managed to make more in a few hours that morning than Fred or Luther or Love had made by a month of work in the field.

The tobacco raisers, standing about in the warehouse and in the street outside, keep talking about government. Men are going through the country now signing them up. The crop is to be cut sharply next year. Government is going to try taking a hand at control in their favor. "It has to begin at the ground, like raising tobacco," Love says. You can't tell these men that prices paid on the floor— in spite of the auctioneer, each company is represented by its own buyer—you can't convince them that the big companies don't fix the price.

Luther, who is more skillful than the others and gets a better price for his tobacco, has a radio and he tells the others what he hears coming through the air at night when he is at home. He speaks about individualism, explaining to the others. "It means something what they call the New Deal. It means that people have got to be made to quit cutting each other's throats. Individualism means that —the devil take the hindermost. We're the hindermost," he says and grins.

On the floor of the great warehouses the sales go on. Men with hand trucks are wheeling away the sold baskets. In another warehouse across the street men are at work packing the tobacco into great hogsheads. A long train of tobacco-loaded cars will leave here tonight. This tobacco, now being sold, may not get to the user for years. It

97

will be handled and rehandled, cured and recured, sorted, graded, tested, treated.

There is a constant hubbub, the cry of the auctioneer, the quick bark of the buyers. The shrewd-eyed pin hookers move from group to group. In the street the patent medicine man keeps talking. "You got hookworms, I tell you."

And now look, it is Fred's turn. The auctioneer and the buyers have come to his baskets. We all go into the warehouse to stand watching, and Fred draws a little away. His old woman, a thin-cheeked one of thirty, already with six kids—they get married young in the mountains—the kids are clinging to her skirts. There is fear in her eyes, in Fred's eyes, and even in the eyes of the children. "You get out of here," Fred says gruffly, and she takes the smallest of the children into her arms and, followed by the others, goes reluctantly away. Fred has spoken gruffly to her, but there is something else back of the gruffness in his voice. He has already had two or three drinks of moon. "You take now your eighteen- or your twenty-cent tobacco—a man can live," Jim says, "but your five- or your six-cent stuff—it's starvation."

Fred walks a little away and I see him standing by the wall. He takes a bottle from his hip pocket and has himself another shot. His best tobacco, his bright lugs, bring nine cents, but all the rest of it, two-thirds of his crop, goes for two and three cents.

Jim, Luther, and Tom do not look at Fred. Luther spits on the floor. Jim steps over and pulls a hand of tobacco out of a nearby basket. "This is pretty good," he says to me. He spreads one of the yellow leaves out over his big hand. "You see, it has been cured right. See how thin it is. Like silk, ain't it?"

The men stand looking at me, and I am suddenly ashamed of my city clothes. Jim, Luther, and Tom all wear patched clothes. Their overalls are patched, and all have long, thin, sun-tanned, wind-bitten faces. "You ain't a government man, are you?" Love asks me again. "Because if you are, you had better tell government they got to keep on helping us what they can."

"We've got pretty puny, trying to help ourselves," Jim says, and they all turn and walk away out of the warehouse and into the street.

"I Want to Work"

"I Want to Work"

I WENT home with a workman from a meeting of unemployed. He had come in there, out of curiosity, as I had. We happened to come out of the meeting at the same time and stopped outside to talk.

The preliminary talk led to another and the next day we met. "Yes, I'm out of work. I'm fifty-two, you see." He was a sturdily-built, clear-eyed man. "I used to make big wages. I should have got fixed for this. I didn't. I was proud, sure of myself, I thought things would always go on as they were. When I did make good money I spent it."

He had been a machinist as a young man and later had become a machine-tender in a factory. He had been out of work for two years. I asked him to come with me to my hotel but he didn't like the idea.

"No," he said, "I'm not dressed for it. You come on home with me."

This was in the early afternoon of a cold day. He was in blue overalls and wore a shabby coat.

His thick, stiff gray hair was only half concealed by his cap. He wore the cap tilted a bit to one side—as though to say—"O. K.—after all I'm as good as the next man."

We went on down to where he lived, stopping at a corner grocer's on the way. "I'll get a few bottles of beer," I said.

"All right. I wouldn't mind having a bottle with you."

I got his story, going down and as we sat in his house. It was an every-day, common enough story.

He had got married as a young man and had one daughter who married a young workman, a machine-fixer like himself. When he was forty his wife died and two years later he got a new wife. He got a young one, nearly twenty years younger than himself, but they had no children.

"They are all at work," he said, "my wife, my daughter, and her husband."

His daughter and her husband had no children. The three of them, his own wife, his daughter, and her husband, had bought a house—it was a small, neat frame house on a little hill beyond a district of huge factories in a Southern industrial town and when we got there we climbed a flight of stairs to a bedroom on the second floor. "You wait and I'll go stir up the furnace and get some glasses for the beer," he said, and when he returned he began to talk—"You see," he said, "I tend to the furnace. I do what I can around here."

He said something, speaking a little bitterly, about what he couldn't do, "I should have been born a woman. If I could cook for the others now. If I could do the family wash, it would save money for them."

You could see that he had been lifted, by circumstances, outside the life of the house in which he had once been the head man.

The point is the way he was taking it. It was obviously the old story of a man whose civilization had got through with him before he was through with it. He had got laid off, when the depression hit the town, and then, later, when his shop started up again, a younger man got his place. "I'm not as fast as I once was," he said, "but I'm a careful man, a good workman yet."

He said he didn't want to offer to work for less wages than the younger man, who has been taken back. "If you begin that," he said, "you cut the standard of a whole shop."

We sat in two chairs by a window that looked down on the factories while we drank our beer and talked. An old feeling, so common in American men, concerned with modern industry—pride in the very thing that has apparently thrown life out of gear.

I have talked to many manufacturers and factory superintendents, and rarely, I think never, have I gone into a shop without being shown some new machine.

Here, in a tin can factory, is a machine that makes can tops. It is the superintendent of the shop showing me through. "When I first came to work here, when I first became a foreman, we had a machine that turned out forty can tops a minute. There was a man at work on every machine. Now you see this long battery of machines. The two men you see walking up and down take care of them all. They don't work so hard. There isn't any heavy work in any modern shop.

"When I was a young man here, a young foreman, I used to go home at night, having seen a new machine installed that would knock out forty can tops a minute. I used to think: 'Are there people enough in the world to use so many tin cans?'" He laughed. "Look at these machines," he said, with pride in his voice. "Every machine in this long row of machines is knocking out three hundred and sixty can tops a minute."

"And you have laid off many men who can never get back into this shop?"

"Yes."

"I do not see many older men."

"No. The younger ones have the call. They are quicker, you see, less likely to get hurt."

I asked him what I have asked many men in positions of control in industry. "When you are all doing it, laying off so many men who can never get back, aren't you laying off your own customers, users of the goods you make here?"

"Yes, we are, all right."

"Well, what are you fellows going to do?"

"I don't know."

That attitude on the part of most of the men in control of the shops. What about the workmen?

Those who say that American workmen, so often now thrown out of their place in our social and economic scheme by the modern machine, so often robbed of something peculiarly vital to their feeling of manhood—this I keep thinking the most important thing of all, the thing I keep hoping that we may come more and more to understand and appreciate——

The machines themselves apparently becoming always faster and faster, more and more efficient—the man in the street can see it with his own eyes in the increased beauty, speed, and efficiency of the automobile——

As though there were actually a kind of devil sleeping down in these so-gorgeously beautiful masses of steel in action——

Those who hold that American workmen do not want to work with the machines, that they do not want to be in the factories, simply do not know what they are talking about.

In the greater majority of American workmen, and now in American workwomen, actual love of the machines and—yes, I am sure of it—in spite of everything—love of the factories. There are, to be sure, always the stupid ones, the dull ones, but the numbers of the other constantly amazes.

The workman, past his prime, who knew what had happened to him and with whom I drank the beer, had got into the habit of going into the public library of the town. As I have said, we were in a Southern town. "I was born a Yank," he said.

"So was I," I said.

His father, a carriage blacksmith, had come South after the war when he was a young boy.

"The kids here used to dog me a lot about being a Yank.

"So I thought, sometime, I thought, when I have time, I'm going to read up on the war.

"I'd never been much to read."

He had got on to one of my own hobbies. "Well," I said.

"Now there was Grant," he said. "I've got to liking that man, at least to liking what he was when he was just a general, before he got to be President. He wasn't such a smart man, but I figure he had the big idea all right."

"Yes? And how?"

"I've been figuring it out. I've got plenty of time to figure things out. A lot of the Northern generals during the war couldn't see the war as a whole. That's what made it last so long."

"You mean?"

"You see, I figure, they thought of a battle as a battle. I think he saw the war as a war."

"He and Lincoln, eh?"

"Yes," he said.

"I've been thinking," he said, "that some day, maybe——

"We may see it as a whole, what we are up against."

I left him sitting in the room and went down the stairs and into the street and on the next day I got into the factory where he had been employed. It was a good one, very modern, very big, light, and efficient.

On the day when I left him and got into the street I wasn't thinking of that.

"They are O. K. They can sure take it," was what I was thinking. And I was thinking that the most pathetic thing of all—in the workman who had been put to one side by his civilization—was his undying so-American optimism.

A Union Meeting

A Union Meeting

I WENT to a union meeting in a mill town. Most of those in attendance were out of work. Every one wanted to talk, and many did. There was reference to the stool pigeon. "We know you're here, stool pigeon. I'm going to say something now. You go and tell Tom Grey." (Tom Grey was the manager of the mill in this town.) It gave you a queer feeling.

I had on a tweed suit and rather loud checked socks, and had been introduced to the meeting by a newspaper man known to be more than friendly to unions. He had told them that I was a city newspaper man. "Anyway, they should know that a stool pigeon wouldn't dress like this," I thought.

The strike is more exciting than just a meeting —it brings out the real leaders. The real leaders are seldom speech-makers. In an amazing number of cases just now, they are rather small, sincere, determined women. Going about among union men and women in America gives you a curious respect for women. They have nerve.

The unions, when they have any, in these Southern industrial towns, meet in curiously depressing halls. The walls are always such an ugly, drab color.

This particular hall had formerly been used by a Ku Klux Klan organization and I asked the newspaper man, "How many of these people were in on that?"

"A good many," he said. He thought the Ku Klux Klan had been rather an outlet for the workers in the days when America was outwardly so prosperous. "The boom market never got down to these," he said, making a sweeping movement with his arm.

Some of these Southern mill-owned towns are rather attractive; good frame houses with green lawns and trees. But not this one. The mill itself, a great brick structure, looked clean and bright. It was, I was told, financially successful, and if you ever have been in such a mill you know the big light rooms, the fast-flying machinery. There was the now so-old contrast—the lives of the workers, the lives of the machines. I like machines. They won't stand being neglected, being made to live dirty, neglected lives. They quit on you.

This one was a big mill, employing a thousand workers, and was owned in the North. All of the employees were of the north Georgia hill-country type. The manager of this mill is also a Northern man. I am covering him up. His name isn't Tom Grey. I'm not telling where his mill is.

During the union meeting, as I listened, there was a curious atmosphere of the back-country, small-town church meeting—references to God— "God wants me to be frank and honest in what I am going to say to you." That sort of thing. I suspected that when Tom Grey talked to his workers, he didn't refer so often to God, but maybe he did.

A delegation had been to see Mr. Grey and the leader of the delegation was to report results. Two other men and a woman had gone with him as members of the delegation.

"We agreed I would do most of the talking. Ain't that right, Sister Smedley? Ain't it right, Brother Small?" the speaker asked. Brother Small and Sister Smedley agreed.

Sister Smedley was attractive. She might have been fifty-five, a thin little old worn woman, with curiously alive eyes. The speaker, the one who had been spokesman for the delegation, was Brother Hadley. Sister Smedley watched him intensely. It was evident that she had taken notes of the conversation with the mill manager. She held a cheap pencil tablet in her hand and fingered it nervously.

"I'll begin at the gate," the speaker said.

"You wait," I whispered to my companion; "in a minute he will begin telling us how he wasn't afraid."

It was a little pitiful to hear. He said that since he had got religion, four years ago, he hadn't lied to any man. "I ain't going to lie to you," he said.

"We were at the mill gate. It was sprinkling a little. There was Sister Smedley, Brother Small, Brother Houseman, and me. It had begun to rain. Now I want to get this straight. It wasn't really raining. It was sprinkling. Am I right, Sister Smedley? Am I right, Brother Small?" Sister Smedley looked quickly at her notebook. "That's right. It was sprinkling," she said. A man sitting near me whispered that Sister Smedley had been in the mill since she was twelve, although she now was an "out." The man said she was a good weaver —"one of the best."

My neighbor was a long, thin man with a long, thin nose, red at the end. He was a loom-fixer.

There had been a strike, the whole mill out, and it had lasted for several weeks. The mill had brought in non-union men, some three hundred of them and when the strike was settled, the manager refused to fire them. The mill took back about seven hundred of the strikers, but there were three hundred left outside, without work.

The union men at the meeting said that the three hundred left outside were their best, their most active union members. The mill management had agreed—"We'll take them back as fast as we can. Whenever any one quits, or gets fired, we'll take back one of the old workers."

There was a persistent cry—"They ain't doing it. They ain't. We want our own people back in there." There was a kind of hesitating, timid desire for loyalty to each other. I was told that most of those at the union meeting that night were outside. Brother Hadley and Brother Small were outside, just as Sister Smedley was.

A collection had been taken for one of the workers. He had been sick and his wife had been sick.

A man got up and reported on his case, not naming him.

"They were pretty near starving down there, so I went to a grocer, Ed Case, it was, and he let me have credit for it, for four dollars and ninety cents.

"So I think Ed Case ought to be paid. I won't tell who it is if he don't want me to tell."

A young workman jumped up. He had been

sitting with his face in his hands, looking at the floor. "It's me," he said. He looked as though he were going to cry. Long-nose told me about him. "He was one of our best speakers during the strike. He was a lot of help, all right.

"You wouldn't think to look at him that he would be a good speaker, but, boy, he is. He's hard to get started, but when he gets started, gets himself worked up, he can go it, I tell you.

"He ought to have been a preacher," Long-nose said. "You can bet Tom Grey ain't going to take him back into the mill."

The report of the delegates who went to see Tom Grey went drearily on. You knew that they had made no progress. There was the tedious story of their getting in, past the mill gate, what the gateman said, what a young man in an office said— "He was one of them young squirts with a pencil in back of his ear."—There was a story of a young woman, evidently Tom Grey's stenographer—"She was scared, wasn't she, Brother Small? Ain't that the truth, Sister Smedley, wasn't she scared?"

It was painfully evident that Brother Hadley had wanted to find some one in the mill office who was scared.

Sister Smedley jumped up. She wiped her thin lips with a thin old hand. This time she spoke in a sharp, frightened voice. "I don't know whether she was scared or not, but I was," she said, and every one laughed.

There was a sense of quick relief in the hall. Sister Smedley sat down and again fingered her notebook. She looked at it. You thought perhaps she had written the words in the notebook, "I was scared." Brother Hadley, who stood upon the little raised platform, swallowed hard and stopped talking to roll a cigarette. His fingers trembled and the tobacco fell in a little shower to the floor.

I turned to my neighbor. "Why was she scared?" I asked. I thought I knew, but wanted to see what he would say. He said he didn't exactly know.

"They've got it on you," he said. "We don't have nothing but our job and they can take it away."

He began a whispered story about Tom Grey, the mill manager. There was the curious thing you find so often among American workers, a kind of understanding of the men over them, a kind of sympathy with a man in Tom Grey's position.

"Maybe I don't blame Tom Grey for being like what he is," Long-nose said to me. Tom Grey, I gathered, had had family troubles. He had a son and two daughters and they had all left him. The wife took the three children and went back up North where they formerly had lived. She never came back.

There had been this delegation, from the workers, going to see Tom Grey. They had been stopped at the mill gate, had been made to stand in a drizzling rain for an hour. Then they were in the office of the plant—They stood in the little hallway. Tom Grey popped out of his office and then popped back in—he didn't speak to them, didn't even look at them.

Sister Smedley jumped up. "I was so mad, I wanted to scream," she cried. Sister Smedley sat down and rubbed her lips.

The tale of the delegation went on. Now they were in Tom Grey's big office. There was a stenographer in there. Tom Grey told her to take down everything they said. "Who are you? What's your name?" he asked each member of the delegation in turn.

Brother Hadley said he had tried to tell him. It was about the workers outside the mill. He said he wasn't a bit afraid. "I talked right out, as plain as I am talking here."

He said Tom Grey had tried to be slick with him. He couldn't chase the old workers who had been in the strike all over town when he needed some help. "I send my foreman to the mill gate. If a worker isn't there and doesn't get hired it isn't my fault."

The mill manager had asked a question, "Do you people represent the outs or the ins? How many members have you got in your dinged old union?" You gathered that he didn't care about the delegation, wasn't much bothered. Obviously, Brother Hadley had talked to Tom Grey as he now was talking to us, hesitatingly, in a half-frightened manner. He had been appointed to do something and hadn't done it.

Now the young man out of work, who had been helped by other union members to the extent of four dollars and ninety cents, stood up suddenly.

"You look in the books," he said. "You'll see that my dues are paid up. I got sick, going and standing at the mill gate in the rain, and Tom Grey, he sent right past me and got men who had never been in the mill before."

The speaker was interrupted by another worker. When the collection had been taken for the man with the sick wife, the second worker had put nothing in the hat.

"I didn't have nothing to put in, Joe," he said, addressing the destitute young worker. "I ain't got no money, but I got canned stuff at home and I got some meal." He asked Joe to come and see him.

On the platform, Brother Hadley had reached the end of his rope. He sat in a chair and tried again to roll a cigarette. When the paper broke again he jumped up and talked rapidly. "I'm one of the outs myself," he said. "We're nearly all out. I was in the other strike we had here six years ago. They got my record. It may be, you ought to have another delegation, another leader, some one else to do your talking. I ain't very good at talking."

He stepped down off the little platform. There was silence in the room. I looked at Sister Smedley, who was still fingering nervously her notebook. I saw something happen. She began to cry silently. Brother Hadley went and stood in the centre of the room, all of us staring at him. There was a queer nervousness.

"I guess we'd better be getting along," the newspaper man said. He also was upset.

"Ain't you visitors going to say nothing to us?" a voice asked.

We stood embarrassed. Brother Hadley was standing in the centre of the room. "I wasn't afraid of him," he said fiercely.

"Why didn't you tell him to go to hell?" a voice cried. "All we want is our jobs."

Several people, men and women, got to their

feet. "I think we ought to hear from Sister Smedley," a woman's voice said. Sister Smedley jumped up. She opened and closed her mouth. "I can't make no report," she said.

The newspaper man and I slipped quietly through the door and out into the darkness of a mill town street. It was raining outside.

New Tyrants of the Land

New Tyrants of the Land

THE South has always been the land of romance to the Americans of the North. It began with most of us in childhood. Some of us remember the men of the Civil War. These men went South when they were young men. They came off Northern farms and out of Northern towns and shops. The war was for them the great adventure. After the war, those who came back returned to rather dull, laborious lives. In imagination afterward they continued to live in fancy the war years. All their lives they kept it up. A whole literature was born. I remember my own boyish imaginings about the South and what happened to me must have happened to millions of Northern boys. When I grew up and for the first time crossed the Mississippi River I was bitterly disappointed and I suffered the same disappointment the first time I crossed the Mason and Dixon Line.

I hardly know what I expected. It was winter and I expected to pass into a land of sunshine, of Negroes singing, of cotton fields, of Southern white men with great beards, riding magnificent horses over their estates. I remember how disappointed

I was to find Kentucky and Tennessee so like Ohio and Indiana.

An illusion of this kind gets into the blood. The average Northerner continues to think of the South as all one thing. It is absurd, but the picture remains.

And I daresay that to the Southerner the same thing has happened. The Northerners are all Yanks. The man of Connecticut is exactly like the man of Iowa. This curious separation of the country into the North and the South is very baffling. It is false. You cannot get the South so—as one picture. There are the plains of Texas and the Tidewater country of Virginia, the upper South with its cotton mills and the great hot Southern basin covering so much of Alabama, Mississippi, South Carolina, and Florida.

The South is like all America—a changing thing. In New Orleans and Mobile the river packets have almost completely disappeared. The old river life is gone. When I first began going South, twenty years ago now, the little packets and some of the big ones still loaded near the banana wharves in Mobile and at the foot of Canal Street in New Orleans. There were the singing, ragged Negro stevedores. Life was fluid and easy. You could go up river from Mobile to Selma and back, a six-

or eight-day trip, for twelve dollars, room and board furnished. You got Negro song, not as you hear it in Northern concert halls, but against a background of river, rain, and woods.

The South is like the North in this—change has swept down on it. If it were ever true that the Southern civilization was pretty much all one thing, men moved by a common impulse, all is changed now. What is there in common between Savannah, Georgia, and Knoxville, Tennessee; between the North Carolina mill section and the sugar bowl of southern Mississippi—down in the deep black belt? What remains is largely an illusion. At Savannah the Southern woman who sits beside you at dinner says, "How can one of you Yanks ever know the South?"

You question her, "Have you ever been in a North Carolina cotton mill at night, in a cypress lumber camp? Have you been in the swamp country, south and west of New Orleans, in the hut of a tenant farmer in Alabama?"

"But these places are not the true South. This is the true South."

In New Orleans, "This is the true South."

In Natchez, Birmingham, Charlotte, "This is the true South."

Within the last year or two Knoxville, Tennessee, has become a new city. The very air of the city has changed. Go from Knoxville to New Orleans, not by the big highways but through the back country. You pass through a dozen civilizations. My father, who was in the Civil War and who afterward talked of it endlessly, always spoke of Southern men, half affectionately, as "Rebs." "So there the Rebs were. They were coming at us out of the woods. They came at us yelling. I tell you, boy, my knees trembled when I saw them coming."

When you are in the South you do not speak of the men of the Civil War as "Rebs" but occasionally the word slips out. You don't speak of the Civil War as a rebellion. You say, "the war between the States." You speak of the soldiers of the Civil War as "Confederates."

The Southerners, however, do not hesitate much about calling you a Yank, and, if you are a Middle Westerner born and bred, that is confusing to you. Let's say you are an Ohio man. You always thought, you were taught as a child to think, of the New Englanders as Yanks. To the Southerner you want to say, "No, sir, and it please you, I'm not a Yank, I'm a Middle Westerner." If you come out of one of the agrarian states of the Middle West, you are constantly baffled and surprised that your own people and the people of the Southern agrarian States do not draw closer. "But yes," you say to yourself, "the agrarian question will not be settled in America for a long, long time. We of the Middle West and the Southerners of the Southern agrarian States should be fighting on the same side. Iowa and Alabama should understand each other. Why are they so separated?" Old hurts last a long time. Both the North and South are still paying for slavery and for the Civil War. Before and after the Civil War the North was so patronizing. We of the North took such a high moral tone when we spoke of slavery.

The Southern story is essentially an agrarian story—a soil story. You are likely to forget that going South now, as many Northerners do go, along the big paved highways through North Carolina, parts of South Carolina, sections of Tennessee, northern Alabama, and Georgia. From Greensboro, North Carolina, to Atlanta, Georgia, along the line of the Southern Railroad, there is one big bright busy industrial town after another. The laborers have been gathered in from the back country. Southern life is changed tremendously in all this industrialized section. You go down through the industrialized upper South, over great smooth cement highways. High Point, Salisbury,

Kannapolis, Concord, Charlotte, Gastonia (but a few years ago the scene of a bitter industrial struggle), Spartanburg, Greenville, Anderson, and on into Atlanta. All day long you drive at top speed and you are never out of sight of the smokestacks of factories.

The towns in all this upper industrial South are pretty much mill-owned. There are bright attractive mill towns and ugly sordid ones. At night the lights from the mills gleam across the hills and across the long flat stretches. The lives of the mill men and women have passed through another swift change during the past year. Nowadays, the mill men and women are free after three-thirty in the afternoon. The streets of the town in the late afternoon are crowded with cars—many new ones these last few months. Now the mill workers, who formerly worked ten and twelve hours a day, have a little leisure. There are plenty of good-looking young girls on the street. They are gaily dressed. Young mill workers are playing baseball on vacant lots.

It should be kept in mind that throughout the whole South the situation of labor is somewhat different from that of the North. The unit of labor is not the man, but the family. In the South you do not rent a piece of cotton land, expecting it to be worked by the man. You expect the wife and the children also to go into the fields. This is true of both the blacks and the whites. It is true also of the cotton mills. Formerly children of ten and twelve worked in the mills, sometimes for ten or twelve hours a day.

More than once in the past year I have cursed the mill owners, and some of the mill managers, often to their faces. A generation ago the towns multiplied like locusts. There was, and is, a deadly sameness to the houses in many of the towns. To the mill owners I have spoken of the long hours, women and children bound to the fast-flying machines for long hours, often at night, the nerve strain, the breaking down of the nerve fiber of children, the wholesale destruction of human material in the mills.

The mill owners always had an answer ready for me. The labor fed into these mills came out of the ranks of the tenant farmers of the South, from the "poor whites" of the hills and the plains. "Go back into the country," a mill manager said to me, "before you complain to us, see what happens there. Look into the lives of the children of the tenant farmers. See what kind of educational opportunities they have, what kind of care they have."

At least in the new industrial towns there were schools. Physically, at least, no State in the Union has such schools as you will find in North Carolina. Among the mill owners a few great humanists sprang up. The work of men like Parker of Greenville, South Carolina, and others of his kind did count. Manufacturers like Harold Hatch did feel their responsibility. Many of the mill villages are bright and charming. When the mills came into many of these Southern towns, they came with song and prayer. In many cases they came into a country worn out by continual cotton-cropping.

The situation of the "poor whites" throughout the entire South is little enough understood in the North. Here was a people that had gone on for generations standing still in a moving civilization. The modern mechanical development of life had barely touched these lives. Modern education had not touched them. They were living in the Middle Ages. When the mills came to some of the towns there were meetings held day and night in the little churches. Prayers went up. "Save us! Save us!" There were cries from many lips, "Thank God! Thank God! It is a new life."

The industrialization of the upper South has gone on rapidly. More and more, people have been gathered into the towns. Although it came some time later, the story of the States of the upper South is also the story of the Middle Western American States. Walk on a Saturday afternoon on the main street of Greenville, in South Carolina, or Greensboro, in North Carolina, and you will have to shake yourself free of the feeling that you are in the streets of some industrialized Middle Western town.

The whole South has got itself divided as the Northern States are divided. There is the industrial South and the agrarian South. Industrialization has come rapidly and swiftly. It is at a pause now. Put the industrial South against the agrarian South and it is like putting Texas against Vermont, the whole huge Russian state against little England. It would be difficult to draw sharp lines. There will be patches of the new industrial South in the great Southern agrarian States. Southern farmers cultivate cotton and tobacco in sight of cotton mills and cigarette factories. There are isolated cotton mills far down in the heart of the agrarian South.

A few weeks ago, I drove for three days with a country doctor in the heart of the Southern cotton country. It was spring, and men were at work in the fields. The country doctor was of a type often met among Southern men. He was poor and lived in a half broken-down house in a quite miserable little Southern town. An old Negro man took care of him. I had heard of him in the town before I went to him. He never sent one of his patients a bill. He was gentle, patient, mentally awake. Lying on the table of his shabby little office I saw a copy of a New York daily. Among the medical books in his library were the works of Balzac, George Moore, Turgenev, Thomas Hardy, and Mark Twain. He was a small man, rather shabbily dressed, the sort of man an organization like the modern KKK would never have dared to fool with. When we met, I said to him, "You are of the best blood of the South, eh?" and he laughed.

"Did you ever know a Southerner who was not of the best blood of the South?" he answered.

I spent some days with the little doctor and he helped to educate me a little. His was a particularly poor section and he was bitter about it. He spoke of the strange new emotional shifts going on in the South just now—the Southerners almost without exception being political democrats. It didn't mean, he said, that they were economic democrats. There was a new emotional alignment.

He spoke of the money-makers of the South, of the men who were first of all money-makers.

"Oh, you have them in the South, too!"

He laughed. In his section, poverty had gone on for a long, long time, ever since the Civil War. It was a country of poor little unpainted, broken-down shacks. As I drove about country roads with him we met shambling, undernourished-looking men, women, and children.

"But are there money-makers in this land, in this country of tenant farmers, among these people, your patients, whites, and blacks?"

"Yes," he said. He had a bitter little laugh. He was a nervous, alive, shrunken old man. I had been told in town that his wife had died young and that he had never remarried. It may very well be that in his little Southern backwoods towns he was the only man who ever looked into a book. The automobile in which we rode was ten years old. "There are men who would make money in hell," he said.

I got from this man, this little country doctor, an inkling of a class springing up and coming into power in the agrarian South. It should be kept in mind that in spite of the rapid growth of industry in some of the upper Southern States, the South, as a whole, is still essentially agrarian. The little doctor thought that in the agrarian South a new type of man was getting to the front. "Even at eight or nine cents a pound, money can be made on cotton if you pay your labor nothing," he said.

He spoke of Negro women picking cotton in his section at thirty cents a day. Often on the land of the new money-making farmer there were no share-croppers or tenants. Whole families were hired for the season. On any big farm in the South there are little shacks stuck on the land, often without floors and windows, one to every twenty-five or thirty acres.

In the back country, the people are desperately poor. They are often without education. Give such a family shelter, just enough money to buy any kind of food, a little corn meal, fat pork, some collard greens—two dollars a week and a house for a family.

Then, if you are hard enough, drive them while they are working for you.

The people thus employed on the land are ignorant, they are in a desperate position. They will take what they can get. They will take anything.

The country doctor thought that there was a new dominant economic class springing up in many of the agrarian States. The new leaders came directly out of the poor, downtrodden class.

Often such a man came from a family that had

been desperately poor. He survived. Life had brutalized him. It had made him indifferent to the sufferings of others. The doctor understood his people. "A man never gets so low in life that he doesn't want to assert his superiority over some one else. If he can't love, then hate becomes a satisfaction," he said.

From the doctor's point of view the new class coming into power in the agrarian South were hard-headed, money-minded people. The older Southern land-owners had felt a sense of responsibility for the people on their land, but the new men did not feel it. Life had driven some of these men mercilessly and now they were becoming drivers. They were buying up land. They could make money on cotton land, no matter what the price of cotton.

It was the doctor's notion that the Southern story was and would remain an agrarian story. Like some of the Southern mill owners, he kept emphasizing the possibilities of brutality on the land. The poorer people, white and black, of the back country, were for the most part ignorant. Often the stores at which these people traded were owned by the land-owner. The books were kept by the land-owner or his clerk. Many of the people could neither read nor write. The cotton allotment would not help most of these people. The more brutal land-owner simply cut down his cotton crop and left the people stranded. Many of the Southern land-owners could not bring themselves to this final brutality of turning the men of the land off the land, but the number of those who could do it was growing. When life has been hard for a man, and he survives, he grows hard.

Later, in another Southern town, I talked to a woman land-owner. There are a good many Southern women now running large farms. The younger men of the families have gone off to the cities, often to the North. I dined with this woman. "If you cut down your cotton acreage," I said to her, "what is to become of the little tenant farmers— those thrown off your land?" "I will take care of mine," she said.

I made my voyage into the South in the late winter and in the spring. Much of my travelling was done in a car on country roads, in the back country. Beside almost every shack there was the broken remnant of a car. The broken-down cars told the story of boom days during the World War. The cars had not been on the roads for years. They were without tires, the tops were in shreds. They were covered with rust. On all the roads broken-down wagons appeared. It was moving time. Tenant farmers were shifting from one hopeless year into another. On each wagon there were a few sticks of broken furniture. Women and children walked in the road behind the wagons. Most of the old mansions, of the old dominant class in the South, were also falling into decay.

I kept thinking of the upper industrial South, of the words the mill managers had said to me—"Go look at the people at home. See how they live there." Travelling through the agrarian South had put the whole problem of the South to me in a new light. I kept thinking of the words of the country doctor, of his description of the new dominant class growing up in the South.

After all, the bigger man, the owner of a cotton mill, or a cigarette factory, is a shining mark. He can be got at. When he is unfair to labor, there he is. President Roosevelt can call such a man into his office, put him on the carpet. He can call into his office the big steel man, the automobile manufacturer, the cotton mill owner. But who is to call to time these hard new little tyrants?

Elizabethton, Tennessee

Elizabethton, Tennessee

To Elizabethton, Tennessee, where there had been a recent flareup of labor trouble among the employees of a huge rayon plant. This is the town so often written up as "the wonder city," "Elizabethton the beautiful," etc. To me it seemed neither very beautiful nor very ugly.

But surely the town is in a lovely place. I had with me a woman engaged with an organization that works for the betterment of the condition of mill women and as we drove down through the beautiful valley toward the town she told me many interesting and sometimes terrible things about the condition of working girls in Southern mill towns.

To me the town, when we got into it, seemed not unlike hundreds of Iowa, Illinois, and Ohio county-seat towns. Earlier there was a period of better building in America. New England felt its influence as did parts of Pennsylvania and all of the South. For some reason these earlier buildings, of stone, brick, and heavy timbers, had more beautiful outlines than the buildings of a later period.

Then followed a period of box construction.

Some one discovered the scroll-saw. Cheap buildings with cheap do-dads on them.

Here is a town that, when I was there, was not more than five years old. Already the buildings had that half-decrepit, worn-out look that makes so many American towns such disheartening places. There is a sense of cheapness, hurry, no care for the buildings in which men and women are to live and work. "The premature aging of buildings in America," said my friend Van Wyck Brooks, "is the saddest thing in America."

We went to the hotel to dine and I went into the washroom. Such places—intimate, personal places —mark a town. The hotel, but a few years old, already had that shoddy, weary air characteristic of cheap, careless construction.

There were a few tiny fragments of cheap soap. The wash-bowls were dirty. Such things are important. They tell a story. "We are not in this place to live. We are here to make money."

We drove out to the two great rayon plants in the evening, just as the employees were leaving. This was mountain white labor. About three-fourths of all the laborers employed were girls.

They were shockingly young. I saw many girls that could not have been beyond twelve or thirteen. In these towns, I am told, children have two ages, the real age and the "mill age." It is easy to escape responsibility. "If she lies about her age," etc.

Of course she lies. These are the poorest of poor people, from the hills, the mountain gullies. They went with weary steps along the road. Many of the young girls were already developing goiters, that sure sign of overwork and nervous debility. They had thin legs and stooped shoulders.

The mills themselves had that combination of the terrible with the magnificent that is so disconcerting. Any one working in these places must feel the power of the mills and there is a sense in which all power is beautiful—and also, to be sure, ugly. Oh, the beauty and wonder of the modern intricate machine! It is said that many of the girls and women in these places are half in love with the machines at which they work.

There is always the old question—to make men rise in nobility to the nobility of the machines.

It is obvious there had not been much nobility in Elizabethton. The girls there were underpaid, they were not organized, they had no power.

A strike flared up, starting I was told, as a kind of spontaneous movement among the girls. It might have been met easily at first. The employers were brutally casual about it.

The girls began to organize and the American

Federation of Labor sent an organizer. His name was Hoffman, a fat man, of the characteristic sledge-hammer, labor-organizer type. A group of men of the town—they had not all been identified yet—went to his hotel at night and escorted him out of town at the point of a gun.

Another bit of characteristic stupidity. He came right back. Such a man would know well the publicity value of such a crude performance on the part of the local business men. It was all nuts for him. Obviously it is true that labor as well as industry and capital has the right to organize. If you own a factory you do not have to employ organized labor if you can get out of doing so. But you cannot stop labor organizing. You cannot throw a man out of town because he comes there to help labor organize. Modern, more intelligent and shrewd industrialists have learned there is a better way to handle such matters. They give labor what it wants. Tack the price on for the buyers at the other end. They throw the burden on over to the consuming public. The middle-class do not know how to organize and apparently the farmers will not organize. And the industrialists are slowly finding out that cheap, underpaid labor is in the end no good.

So here were these girls organizing and the

movement grew like wildfire. The men came in. All Elizabethton was apparently being organized. Later, as almost always happens, it all fell to pieces.

There is one thing about being a writer. You can go anywhere. Had I not written a book called *Poor White?* It was the industrial history of a town very like Elizabethton. And I had written *Winesburg, Ohio,* stories of the private lives of poor people in small towns.

I myself came from the working class. When I was a young man I worked in factories. These working people were close to me, although I was no longer a working-class man. I had my own class. I kept looking and wondering. Occasionally I tried to put down in words what I saw and felt.

And here is a peculiar thing. I am thinking now of working women. I take it that all women want beauty of person. Why not? How often I go to dine, for example, at one of the hotels in my own town. There are the guests coming in. We, in my town, are on the Lee Highway. Many women come here. They are rich women, going South to Florida, or returning to the North from Florida. They are dining at the hotel.

How few of them have any grace of person, any grace of body. I look from these women to the working women, the waitresses. How much nicer they seem.

It is true everywhere I have been. In the great fashionable hotels a man does sometimes see beautiful young girls but the older people among them are usually quite miserable looking. I mean they are usually smug, self-satisfied about nothing, without character. Hard work, trouble in life does, it seems, after all beautify, to one with an eye at all trained to see beauty.

A moment ago I spoke of my own position in life. I am accepted by working people everywhere as one of themselves and am proud of that fact. The other evening in Elizabethton there was a secret union meeting being held. I went up into a rather dirty hallway, crowded with girls. "Perhaps this Mr. Hoffman has read some of my books," I thought, "he may let me in here." There was no doubt about the woman I had driven to Elizabethton. They would let her in. And so I sat in a window-sill and along came this man Hoffman, the labor organizer. "Hello, Sherwood Anderson," he said. "Do you want in here?"

"Yes, of course. I want in everywhere. To go in is my aim in life. I want into fashionable hotels and clubs, I want into banks, into people's houses, into labor meetings, into courthouses. I want to see all I can of how people live their lives. That is my business in life—to find out what I can—to go in."

I did not say all this. "Sure," I said.

And so I was escorted into a room packed with girls, with women, boys, and men.

It was a business meeting of this new trades organization, a certain local of the Textile Workers of America.

There were girls everywhere. What a different looking crowd from the one I saw, but two hours ago, coming from the factories.

There was life in this crowd. On the evening I was there some fifty new members were sworn into the organization. They came forward in groups, awkward young girls, awkward boys, men, and women with prematurely old faces, not tired now, full of life. As each member was sworn in, applause shook the room. A woman was outside who had no money to join. "I'll pay for her," cried a working man, coming forward out of the crowd. He put his hand into his overall pocket and slapped the money down on a table.

More and more men and women were crowding up the narrow hallway outside. They wanted to join. The crowd laughed, jokes were shouted about the room. "Why, there's Red. Hello, Red. Are you in?"

"You bet I am in."

There is a report that the company is going to fire all those who join. "Well, then we will go back to the hills. I lived on birdeye beans before there was any rayon plant and I can live on birdeye beans again."

At least there was joy in this room. Men and women, for the time at least, walked with new joy in their bodies. The men became more dignified, more manly in their bearing, the women more beautiful.

And many of these mountain girls are lovely little creatures. They have, at least when excited, straight hard little bodies, delicately featured faces. I sat beside a child that couldn't have been over thirteen—no matter what her "mill age"—and as I looked at her I thought how proud I would be to have been her father.

I felt that way about all of the people in the room. Those working men I could accept as brothers, those girls as sisters. They were and are closer to me, as are men everywhere who work in fields, in factories, and shops, than any other class of men or women will ever be.

And who loves luxury more than myself.

It is very puzzling. I came away from Elizabethton puzzled. How will it all come out?

"At least," I thought, "these working men and women have got, out of this business of organizing, of standing thus, even for the moment, shoulder to shoulder, a new dignity. They have got a realization of each other. They have got for the moment a kind of religion of brotherhood and that is something."

It is a great deal more than any wage increase they may win from their struggle.

They had built a monument in Elizabethton. It was at the head of the main street. I fancy they felt that the town should have a monument. Almost all towns have. Perhaps also there was nothing in particular to build a monument about. Apparently they just built one anyway. I walked around it several times but could find no inscription on it. It was built of brick with a thin outer coating of cement. Already it was falling to pieces. How I would have liked to see one of those delicately featured, hard-bodied, little mountain girls, done in stone by some real artist, standing up there on the main street of that town.

"Please Let Me Explain"

"Please Let Me Explain"

On the road I saw many people trying to catch a ride. There were old men and young men, some of them quite respectably dressed and others in rags. I saw two different families, father, mother, and children, with little packs on their backs tramping the roads. I had goods in the back of my car and had room but for one passenger at a time. I picked up two men, carrying one of them a part of the way, dropping him at his destination, then picking up another. The first was an old man, respectably dressed, like a well-to-do working man of ten years ago and with a little gray mustache. He told me that five years ago he was a big wheat farmer in the West. He had a good deal of land but wanted more and so he went into debt at the bank and bought more land. He owed money at the bank and could not pay. The price of wheat fell and fell. The bank examiner came to his town and told the bank they had to get rid of their frozen assets. The man was sold out. "In my section," he said, "at least seventy-five per cent of the farmers will be sold out unless things change and change quickly." The man never had any children but he and his wife had adopted children. His wife is dead. He has had to throw his children back upon their own people who are, he told me, very poor. "I have become a common workman," he said, "but who wants me?" The man was strong and alert at sixty-five but who nowdays wants a workman of sixty-five?

Every man and in particular every American is anxious to tell you his life history. He wants to explain himself.

In America every man who is broke, down on his luck, is half ashamed of the fact. Everywhere now you see people who are not yet broke. They have possessions. They have not lost their farms or their stores or their houses. In spite of the depression they may still have some money left. Perhaps they are ashamed, too. It may be that nowdays all of us who are not entirely broke and see people everywhere in destitution are a little ashamed of our own safety. We have an inclination to say—"The fellow could get a job if he wanted to work." It makes us feel better. Or we say—"Look at these fellows. Nearly all of them own automobiles."

We forget how it was here in America a few years ago, in times of prosperity. Then every man who had a job and any kind of an income and who didn't own an automobile was driven almost crazy by high pressure salesmen. Radio salesmen were after him, automobile salesmen, refrigerator salesmen. He was made to feel that he wasn't any man at all unless he went in debt for a car or for a radio. All the big men in American life cried out constantly—"Spend. Spend." Well the poor fellow did it. Now he has the car and owes money for it. He can't run it and he can't sell it. The position of the American in times like these is somewhat different from the position of any other man in the world. That should be borne in mind.

For example let us compare him with the European man. In Europe the common man does not expect ever to rise in the world. The man is born into a certain position in life and in ninety-five cases out of a hundred he stays there. Let us say the man's father owns a little wine shop or a grocery store or is a small farmer, a land owner. The son expects to follow in his father's footsteps. He doesn't expect to rise in the world and others do not expect him to rise. To be sure there are exceptions. Men of extraordinary energy or genius do arise and push themselves forward. But such men are rare. The man whose father owns a little wine shop inherits the wine shop when his father dies, but he doesn't begin thinking—"how can I make my wine shop bigger?" He doesn't begin scheming to own a dozen wine shops. His father lived in a certain way and he in turn fully expects to live in the same way, is quite content usually to live that way. For example, I have been going to Europe every five or six years now for perhaps twenty-five years. I always go to Paris. In the Rue Jacob in Paris there is a certain little wine shop. There are rows of wine bottles upon shelves running from the floor to the ceiling. The man now running that shop is about my own age. His father ran it and his grandfather. It was never smaller than it is now and perhaps never will become any larger. The man knows personally every customer who comes into his shop. He even remembers me. If, after five years, I go into his shop again, as I always do when I go to Paris, he looks up and smiles. "Hello," he says. "You are back here. You are looking very well. You haven't been here for a long time."

He has a son who will in turn some day run the shop but no one is telling the son that when his time comes he should hustle to make the shop bigger, that he should live in a larger house than the one his father lived in or that he should be in any way anything bigger and grander than his father and his grandfather. You can see, of course, that this fact gives the son a certain solid feeling about life. He is a man who has his roots in the place where he was born. The fact gives him a kind of strength that is good to see. The man will not always have to be explaining himself to every one. "I am the keeper of a wine shop," he says, or, "I drive this dust cart." I have seen men going along the road in European countries driving carts that it was good to see. There the man went along the road. He had his whip under his arm. His hat was cocked on the side of his head. There was even a strut. "Well, look at me if you want to. I am here driving this cart. I am a cart driver. What of it?" Even the very beggars in some of the European countries have this air.

On the other hand there is the American. He can't, of course, be like that. It is a very queer thing but the truth is that we Americans, who talk so proudly of our individuality and of our independence, are always going about explaining ourselves. It is easy to see how it came about.

We Americans have all been taught, from childhood, that it is a sort of moral obligation for each of us to rise, to get up in the world. I am sure there must be thousands, perhaps millions, of Americans whose experience in this respect has been like my own. Progress. Progress. That was the cry.

161

We were all taught that there is a certain kind of disgrace in being poor. How sharply I remember how the men of my own town spoke to me when I was a lad. The mayor of the town did it, the merchants did it, the judge spoke to me, a preacher spoke to me. I was a rather energetic, hustling boy. I was strong, cheerful, and willing. I wasn't afraid of work. I have become lazier since.

"Good boy. Be a hustler. Go after it. That's right. Make money. Money makes the mare go," they said.

There it was, right from the beginning. You had to have money to rise in the world, to be a bigger, showier man than others in order to respect yourself. Of course, every man wants to respect himself. Money was the outward sign of inner merit. Men are still judged in that way in America. I must suppose that some of the men that spoke to me thus at that time, for example the preacher, the judge, and others, did not exactly mean what they were saying. It was easier, more simple, to put it in that way and then I must suppose, too, that in an earlier day in America, when the country was being built up there was a kind of merit in being always active, always on the go, a hustler. If you had got money men could judge you easier. "He has accumulated money. He must be all right." It was the easier way of passing judgment.

It is always, of course, easiest to judge the merits of any man's work by physical facts. Here is a man who has built the highest building in the world, made the most automobiles, has driven an airplane or an automobile faster than any other man, is the richest man in the world. By the American standard that man is, almost automatically, a man of merit. It is obvious.

But now we Americans have been caught up with. The newspapers, the politicians who want to get into office and others are telling us that the depression we are now in is only a temporary thing. The chances are, however, that it is something more than temporary, that it may become permanent. There are a good many signs nowdays that we are at the end of one stage of civilization and must pass into another. A good many men think that what must pass is the age of capitalism, that some of these days soon now all of the great trusts, the chain stores, the big mills, and factories and even the land must be taken over by the State. The age of individual opportunity to accumulate may be passing and if this is true it is going to be hard for the American to adjust himself.

If you do not think this is true, the next time

you are on the road pick up one of the Americans now down and out. Talk to him in a friendly way. See how quickly he begins to explain himself, to apologize. It may be that he has nothing to do with the circumstances that have put him where he is but just the same he feels guilty. He does not blame his civilization. He feels that in some way he is not a good American because he has not risen above his fellows.

There is the wheat farmer who for a few years was a prosperous farmer. Now he is down and out. He is old and knows he cannot get work. He was going to live with some of his dead wife's relatives and was ashamed. He needed little encouragement from me to begin explaining himself. Although he had worked hard all his life, raising food for people to eat, he was in no way indignant about what his civilization had done to him. He should have been smarter, shrewder, should have taken more advantage of other men. "It's my own fault," he said, "I was not smart enough." It is the average American's point of view yet and it is a little hard to contemplate. You would think in times like these men would be actively thinking and planning for the future. If it is true, as some of us now think, that we are coming to the end of one age, and going into another, you would think that every one here would be planning for the future—that our big men would be submitting plans—that we would all be thinking and working to make all life here better for all of us, but, as a matter of fact, nothing of the sort is being done yet by Americans. Only a few people—and they are not called good Americans—seem to be making any plans at all for the future. Most of them are as yet considered crazy and dangerous people.

However, yesterday, when I was driving on the road after I had picked up my first man and taken him to his destination, I picked up a second man who did have a plan. It wasn't his own plan. It was a thing he thought would happen. He was a young man and looked as though he had been ill. He was rather shabbily dressed. I picked him up at the edge of a town and he told me that he had been going through the town trying to sell to some one for twenty-five cents a pocket knife he still had in his possession. He wanted to get the money to buy himself something to eat and I tried to talk to him to see if he had any plan for the future in America.

He said he had been thinking it over. He said he thought that the rich in America and the well-to-do people here would presently pass a law. He said he expected it would be done, that he looked forward to seeing it done. He said he thought that the poor and the unemployed in America would have to be killed. It was, he thought, the only way out. He said he had thought about it a good deal. He was a rather sensitive-looking man.

"But you would be one of the first to be killed," I said.

"I know, but," he said, "you see I haven't succeeded. I don't believe I ever will succeed," he said. "I might as well be put out of the way."

It is, as yet, I suspect, about the average American point of view. It is simple. It would no doubt be easier than tackling the terrific problem of what we are to do with America and Americans in the new age that is apparently coming.

The Nationalist

The Nationalist

WHAT charms you about all of this travelling about America is not the scenery but the people met. I met a nationalist on a train coming out of New Orleans. We were both bound for New York. It was at the height of summer and his face was red as my own. Drops of sweat stood on his broad forehead and little rivulets of sweat ran down his fat cheeks. There were few passengers and I found him sitting alone in the lounging car at the end of the train. A conversation began at once and I told him I was a writer.

It is a good plan. He was so evidently a successful business man, and successful business men are curious about writers. For a moment he looked at me, I thought with suspicion in his eyes, and then something, no doubt my easy grace of manner, my eagerness to be social—I had on a good, conservative suit of clothes—he decided to expand.

He began by giving me a cigar. "Don't be afraid," he said. "It's a good one." It was.

"And do you write for the popular magazines?"

"Sometimes," I said. I did not tell him how infrequently.

He expanded more and more.

"There is no doubt that he is an important man," I thought. There was even a kind of melting not caused by the heat. He had small gray eyes and they looked at me eagerly, even a little greedily.

He began at once to tell me his story, the story of his adventures in life. All Americans do that, and it developed that he was a rat man. At first I didn't understand. "I am in the rat game," was what he said. I knew at once that he would be at the top of any game he was in. Presently it developed that he was in reality a rat king and, again looking at him, I began to think that he would inevitably be one of our American kings.

Everything was explained carefully, elaborately. We had plenty of time. By rats he meant the muskrat, a rodent I had known in my boyhood.

The muskrat used to live along the creeks in my Ohio country and I had seen him there. As I remembered him, he was nearly as large as a cat. His pelt had a certain value. As a boy I had known another boy who set traps for him.

"Oh, yes. I know. I understand now."

But I did not understand. It was obvious that this man, with his air of command—there was something in his manner not unlike an army general—with a certain large assurance and confidence in self

—could be no setter-out of muskrat traps, skinner of muskrats, simple dealer in the pelts of rats. "This man has not got to where he is buying pelts from country boys such as I used to know," I thought.

He was however explaining, and at once he differentiated between the Northern and the Southern muskrat. Like a good many Northern men who come South, he was more Southern than the Southerners. He spoke with a kind of contempt of Northern rats, saying that they were over-valued. For a long time there had been a notion abroad that the Northern rat was superior. "It is all nonsense," he said. I gathered that he personally had had much to do with a gradual change he said was taking place in public opinion.

As for the Southern rat it had its home, its paradise, in certain swamp lands near the city of New Orleans. A great many people had a misconception of the city and where it stood. They thought it was at the mouth of the Mississippi River, but it wasn't. It was more than a hundred miles from the river's mouth and stretched away on the east and the west, far to the east and far to the west, where there were thousands, even millions, of acres of swamp lands. "Oh, yes," I said. I had heard that.

What I did not know about was the great rat industry that had gone on for years in these swamps. There were these millions of acres of swamps and more millions of rats lived in them. There had been an industry built up. All through these swamps, he explained, there were people living. The rats lived in the swamps and these people lived upon the rats. They were trappers, living in the swamps. Their houses were built upon stilts stuck in the ground. They lived in boats.

"The Cajans," I said. "Yes," he replied.

It happened that I knew something of these swamps.

"It is where the mosquitoes come from," I said, and he laughed.

So there were these people who lived in the swamp lands. They were trappers. They spoke a bastard French I gathered that for a century or more they had lived thus, in the swamps, not owning the swamp lands, paying each a small sum each year to the owners of the land. Although they were poor, they were an independent and a proud people.

And then the rat king had appeared. I do not know whether or not the man I met on the train was the actual king. He told of what had been done, but he spoke in the plural. "We did so and so," he said.

II

The swamp lands had been acquired. There had been a company formed. The central idea, I gathered, had really been the welfare of the rats in the swamps and the trappers in the swamps. A company had been formed and millions of acres of the half-submerged lands had been acquired.

There had been a struggle. The trappers in the swamps had been gathered in and everything had been explained, but at first they had not understood. It was not for the good of the trapper or the rat that things go on as they were. These men had been too independent. Each man paid his yearly sum and went as he pleased into the swamp. He set traps as he pleased.

It had all been carefully explained, the man on the train told me, but the trappers were very stupid men. "Now you will no longer work for yourself. You will work for us." The land would be divided and subdivided. "You may put your house here or there. We will say where you may put your house. We will lay out your trap line for you. Life will no longer be a gamble. You will not go on as you have done, in this uncertain way. You will now work for wages.

As for the Southern rat, I gathered that he needed protection. There were certain years when the salt waters from the gulf came up into the swamps and the rats died by the million. Places of refuge had to be provided. There were certain men among the trappers who caught rats too early or too late in the season. It was odd that the trappers did not, would not at first understand all that was being done for them. There had been a long and bitter struggle but in the end the rat company, headed by the rat king, had won.

There were other things to be taken into consideration. The Southern rat had never been properly publicized. He was like so many other outstanding features of the Southern civilization. The Southern rat had been looked down upon. The man on the train became charming in his whole-hearted defense of the Southern rat and in his concern for Southern civilization. With his big hand he pounded upon the seat of his chair and his jaw became set.

"You'll see," he declared, "the time will yet come when the Southern rat will come into his own!"

He explained to me many things that could be done with the Southern rat. It had to be caught, to be sure, at just the right season of the year.

"This business," he said vehemently, "of allowing a lot of selfish individual men to run about over the swamps!" They took everything from the rats and gave nothing back. You could not allow a matter of such great importance to the whole South to remain in the hands of individuals. They caught the rats too early in the season or too late. The pelts were not treated as they should be. In the hands of experts in such matters the Southern rat could become anything. It could become mink, or otter, or even beaver. The future of the Southern rat was something tremendous.

The man whom I took to be the rat king of the South explained everything to me. Now that the rat industry was being controlled, everything was being thought of. In reality, for example, the flesh of the Southern rat was delicious. There was a good deal of prejudice about eating rats, but it was all nonsense. It was like the American prejudice against eating snails. The French did it. They found the snail a delicious morsel. Experiments were being conducted to change the flavor of the rats. They could be given the flavor of the most delicious fish or even of venison.

The man on the train came near weeping, thinking of all this.

"Think of it," he said, "all of these tons of delicious food wasted. And men often going hungry, too," he said.

He said that there were certain difficulties to be overcome. There were the so-called pure food laws. A lot of silly reformers had got at Congress. "The flesh of the Southern rat is delicious," he said again. He smacked his lips. "These damn reformers," he said.

He looked steadily at me.

"You have no use for such people have you?" he asked.

"I think they are very un-American," I said, and "You are damned right," he agreed.

III

He had got now upon the subject of laws. He himself was a law-abiding citizen, but there were certain laws, laws put through by the least American of our people. Did I ever go to Washington? "You writers," he said. He thought we writers must have a certain influence.

He became more and more in earnest. It was evident that a new thought had come to him.

"There is something else," he said. He looked about the car. A small and aged woman in black had come into the lounging car, but she sat far away. He lowered his voice. There was, he said, a matter he thought he should speak to me about. There was my position as a writer. No doubt I had friends. There was a law that had been put on the statute books that was hurting him and his company.

It concerned, he said, a thing called egrets. Did I know what an egret was? "Aha!" He thought not. The egret was a bird. It was a mischievous and terrible bird. "Look at us," he said. "We have fish hatcheries all over the country. The egret lives on fish."

The egret, he declared, was a bird that did not belong to America. It was not an American bird.

Still it came here. It came in thousands into the land he and other good Americans had acquired. It did not come, he said, to live in America. It came only to breed and it happened that this particular bird—it had a peculiarity—at the time when it was setting on eggs and brooding its young—the young would not stay in America when they grew old enough to fly—they would fly away to South America—they were really South American birds——

And it happened that these birds—at just a certain time—when they were brooding these foreign youngsters—at that time there were feathers that grew on them, very delicate and beautiful feathers —women liked to wear them on their hats. He said that he did not blame the women.

"I think that our American women are the most beautiful women in the world," he said. "I would deprive them of nothing."

But it had happened. A lot of women reformers —they were probably old maids—they had done it. A law had been passed.

"We cannot shoot these birds," he said. "If we could shoot them they would bring us in thirty to forty dollars apiece."

"It isn't the money I am thinking about," he said. There was a grave injustice being done. "These egrets," he said again, "are not American birds. They are foreign birds and they come up here only to eat our American fish."

He thought that I, being a writer and if I were a good American, should do my part to correct such a glaring injustice.

"You have friends," he said. "You could ask them to write to their Congressmen."

He gave me another cigar.

"Will you try to do something about it?" he asked, and I promised I would.

"I will write about it some day," I said and, "That will be splendid!" he cried.

He said that nothing made him so sad as the thought of these millions of native American fish gobbled up each year by these damned foreign birds.

They Elected Him

They Elected Him

To an older man, any older man, going into West Virginia any time within the last three or four years, there would have come at once a prejudice: "Who is this Rush Holt, every one in West Virginia is talking about?"

"So here is another of these 'flash' young men." Such young men, often by circumstances thus pushed up, these young Napoleons! The older man remembers that it was in the hills of West Virginia that the young George McClellan got his start as a warrior, the young McClellan who later, hailed as a young Napoleon, was suddenly pushed up to command of the Army of the Potomac. How it all went to his head. He was the great one. He kept Abraham Lincoln waiting in the hallway of his house. "I haven't time to see him now. I'm busy." A few quite amazing victories in the hills of West Virginia early in the war, and then that. Will the same thing happen to Rush Holt?

It is a fair question because what Rush Holt has done in West Virginia is something new in American affairs, and certainly new in West Virginia.

183

Do you know West Virginia? You should. It is one of the most interesting states in America.

It is a land of mountains and swift-flowing rivers, of big water-power companies, gas, oil, and coal.

Coal, plenty of coal.

They have been taking it out of the West Virginia hills by the millions of tons, shovelling it out, using the latest mining machinery, blowing it out of the hills by the acre, any way to get it out quickly and at the lowest possible cost.

Plenty of good mines ruined when they were but half worked out, plenty of men killed in the mines because of cheap, hurried timbering. The waste of power and wealth in coal in the country is like the huge land waste in America. It is one of the crimes of America. Any man who travels over this country and does not see everywhere the necessity for a new regimentation is blind. Individual liberty means, too much, liberty to destroy.

Although West Virginia is a land where millionaires have been made rapidly, coal, oil, gas, water-power, lumber, and industrial millionaires, it has also made plenty of poverty. There are a hundred thousand coal miners in West Virginia, men in the big mines, the little mines, the wagon mines. A few years ago around Weston, where this new man, this new West Virginia leader, Rush Holt, came from, they struck gas. It was so plentiful and so cheap that for a time, for a few years, they sold it to you for twenty-five cents the fire. You turned it on, left it on, threw the windows open to cool the house. What difference did it make. The biggest, highest-powered gas well ever blown off in America was blown off near Weston.

Go into West Virginia now and they'll tell you. Older men will tell you an old American story of the days of the opening up of the country—the coal mines being opened up, one after another, each new mine bigger than the last, the water-power companies coming, old Mother Earth belching forth her gas, the old lady being more and more wounded and hurt. Blood flowing out of her wounds.

On every side new millionaires being made. Get yourself a piece of mountain land. Dig down into it, bore down. You may be the lucky one. This is a free country. Every man has a chance here.

Over in the neighboring coal and power State of Pennsylvania they had the same thing but also something else. In Pennsylvania there was always the background of solid German and Dutch farmers. Drive west from Philadelphia into the land over about Lancaster and York. It is one of the sweetest, richest farming sections in America and every year it grows richer.

But there is nothing like this in West Virginia. It is a land of riches and poverty. Never, in all my wanderings over America, have I seen such desolate towns. They send a shudder down the spine. "Are children raised in these black holes?" you ask yourself. "Do boys and girls grow into manhood and womanhood here?" You stop your car on one of the paved highways above such a town. There is the mine, that black hole in the side of the mountain above the road. Coal, thousands of tons come roaring down a runway to the tipple. Below there is a river and the rivers of West Virginia are very beautiful and beside the river a mining town. Often such a town will be quite empty, the mine worked out, the houses, so poorly, so shabbily built, in the beginning, now with roofs sagging and the doors and windows gone.

But you have stopped by a town still occupied, a mine still being worked. There is a railroad along the bank of the river, below the town, and beside the railroad, a long row of coke ovens.

The coke ovens are pouring forth black smoke. The wind blows it down over the town. It lifts and falls. Although you have stopped your car within a few hundred yards of the spot where the town used to be, the town itself is often quite wiped out. Only a dense cloud of black smoke lies over the place where it once stood.

It is a matter of black wonder to the man out of the open country, away from these hills. He keeps asking himself—"Can ordinary human life go on here, in this black land!" It does. Now the smoke lifts. So life goes on here as in any American town, a little clean New England town or an Iowa corn-shipping town. See, it is fall now and a group of boys—half men, in their football togs are in a vacant lot running off football signals. Red Jacket, home of the famous Yellow Dog Contract, will be playing the schoolboys of Mateawan next Saturday. Laughter and cries out of the black smoke down there.

Here comes a young man, a young miner, down a path in the scrubby wood that leads up into the hills, his arm about the waist of a young woman. They'll tell you these West Virginia miners are not Americans. It's a lie. Many are American to the bone.

The onlooker remembers stories he has been hearing, stories picked up from the lips of coal miners in company stores, in a coal miners' house where three or four big-bodied miners sat smoking their pipes about the kitchen stove after the day in the mine. "How about a little more of that beer, Jake?" Stories of fights in the mines, on the streets of the mining town. Stories of the old Hatfield-McCoy feud of Mingo and McDowell counties, over on the Tug River, at the edge of Kentucky, land where almost every man you met on the streets of a mining town went armed. Men shooting their way into power. Men keeping power with shotguns and rifles. "We were lying up above town in the hills, when the thugs came down the railroad track we gave it to them. We got eight."

Strangers coming into such a town, travelling salesmen and others were often stopped on the street. Or a merchant told such a one, "Say stranger, let me tell you something. If you've got any opinions keep them to yourself. Keep your mouth shut while you are in this county."

The young man, Rush Holt—now suddenly pushed up, largely by labor, to be the outstanding leader in West Virginia. His first name is Rush— he is aptly named—he's a fast one all right, has been fast since he was born, twenty-nine years ago. He did not come out of a mining town, but out of the rolling hill country some hundred and fifty miles northeast of Charleston, up near the Pennsylvania line. His people, on both his father's and mother's side, have been there in that country a long time. They were there and Weston was an old town before the Civil War, when West Virginia was a part of old Virginia. Old Virginia built a huge stone hospital up there. West Virginia wasn't so rich then. The forests hadn't been cut away, but few of the mines had been opened.

It was a land of hill people, and here is something interesting. Hill people are proverbially an independent proud people and coal miners are not meek. There is nothing of the pale factory hand about your coal miner. In the first place, the very nature of the miner's work makes him a proud, a highly individual man. The miners do not work in large gangs, under the eye of a boss, but commonly by twos, in little rooms down under the ground. They work always in the face of danger. Each man must depend absolutely on the courage and coolness of his fellow. See the miners coming out of the mines at evening. Their faces are black. The coal miner's lamp is in the caps. There are white men and Negro men, now all black. See them as they walk in the streets of their towns. "Go to the devil. I'm a man. I do a man's work. Just because I am black and dirty and do black dirty work, don't expect me to kowtow to you." Between the native mountain man and the coal miner there is something in common and, for that matter, a great many of the West Virginia coal miners come out of the hills.

And so there they are, the coal miners, and there are the Holts of Weston. The Holts are a tall, lean, good-looking race. And what striking individuals. Rush Holt's grandfather, although he was a Virginian, was a Northern sympathizer when the Civil War came, but when his son, Matthew Holt, ran away from home and enlisted in the Northern army at thirteen, then the old man went and jerked him out. "If you are going to fight, I'll tell you who and when to fight."

"Yes, you will not. I'm only thirteen now, and you can get me out of this war, but I'll find my own wars."

He did. Rush Holt's father, Doctor Matthew Holt of Weston, West Virginia, has been in a fight ever since. Now he is the independent mayor of the town of Weston. The Civil War is the only fight in a long life he has missed. He became a doctor and didn't marry until he was forty-eight. His son Rush, at twenty-nine, isn't married yet. He'll be a catch when he gets to Washington, this young Senator.

And I dare say that almost every normal town in America has a character like Matthew Holt. He would have lived, until he was forty-eight at the town hotel. He was a doctor and a good one, and all day rode around the country, curing people and getting into arguments. He would have read Bellamy's *Looking Backward* and the books of Bob Ingersoll. As he spent most of his days driving about the country in a horse and buggy, he would have become a bit horse crazy.

"Well, why not. I'm not married and have no kids. I make money. Why not spend it on horses?" He would have been fond of fast trotters, and had some good ones in his stables, taking them about the country to the county fairs.

And when not driving a fast horse, he would engage in an argument, in the town drugstore or on the courthouse steps.

He would have been the sort of man who got into every fight that ever started in that fighting country. Like his son Rush, he would have been a smiling fighter, not hating the men he fought, never hating. What is the use wasting energy in hating? A country doctor finds out about other men. He is engaged in a bitter fight with Jim Smith today—the fights are always about ideas— Doctor Matthew Holt, an old man now, would have been strong for woman's suffrage before the women of his town had ever heard of it. He would have been for birth control before Margaret Sanger was born—he is in a bitter fight with Jim Smith today but tomorrow night Jim's baby will be taken ill suddenly, and there is Doctor Holt by the bedside. There is something nice in his voice now.

"Take it easy, Jim. Don't worry. We'll pull her through."

Such a man, well-hated sometimes, sometimes deeply loved. When the World War came on, he was already an old man, married now and the father of six children—his wife, the Scotch woman, Chilela Dew—the Dews also a professional family, all school teachers, or doctors, or judges—a great-aunt of Rush Holt's was the first woman in West Virginia to pass the State medical board and to get a license to practice medicine in the State—when the World War came on, old Doctor Holt was against it. He saw it then as we all see it now. He fought openly against it and one night, when he was returning from the bedside of a patient, a mob set upon him. He had his wife with him in his car, she also was an old woman now, and one of the rocks, thrown by the mob, clipped her on the head. It didn't kill her. They don't kill easily in that family.

But the old doctor didn't quit fighting, and he had help. A crowd of men came to the front.

They didn't agree with the old doc, but he was the old doc. Tall men from the hills came down with their rifles and marched up and down before his house. They set a guard over him and his house. "We don't agree with your damned opinions, doc, but you go on fighting. We'll stand by you." It was Voltaire's pronouncement taking an American form. "I don't agree with a damn word you say, doc, but I'll fight for your right to say it."

The doctor, Rush Holt's father, did keep on fighting, sometimes having the whole town with him and sometimes having it against him. He fought the gas companies, the power companies. Only two years ago, at eighty-four, he put up for Mayor. He wasn't on either the Democratic or Republican ticket. "All right. I'll run. If you want me for Mayor, write my name on the ticket." They did. He got more votes than the two regular candidates combined.

I have already said that young Rush Holt was fast. I rode with one of his brothers in a car. We went along over the mountain roads at sixty but he apologized to me. "Rush drives faster than I do," he said.

Rush was out of high school at fourteen and went down to the University of Cincinnati. He was wearing short pants yet and they wouldn't take him, but the University of West Virginia would. They thought, down at Cincinnati, that he was too much the child.

They thought the same thing when he got into the State Legislature and also when, at the request of the workingmen of his State, he put up for the Democratic nomination for Senator. In the newspapers of the State, they put cartoons showing him riding about in a kiddy-car. A newspaper man at Charleston told me an amusing story.

"When he first came down here, to the State Legislature," said the newspaper man, "—most of the newspapers of the State had been either against Rush or had been mild supporters in the fights he had made in the State—fights against the power companies and the big corporations—but the newspaper men, the leg men, have been for him to a man—the newspaper man laughed—"he came down here and there was a question of seats on the floor of the House. Rush went to the man who arranges about the seats. 'I want to be up front. I guess I'll be doing quite a lot of speaking,' he said."

That and the other story—when he was swept into the Democratic nomination for the United States Senate, defeating seven other older and more experienced political figures. They told him he couldn't get into the United States Senate.

"You have to be thirty, and you will be only twenty-nine."

"Oh, I don't know," he said. Henry Clay got in at twenty-nine."

It is a laugh. It is something good. My own impression of Rush Holt, got before I ever saw him, on other trips into West Virginia, when he was being talked of in the State—wasn't very favorable. "So, another young genius," I said to myself. "Very likely he'll be a young smart-aleck."

Then I went and watched him at work on the floor of the Legislature of his State. I went unannounced to some of his political meetings. I followed him into the rough country, into McDowell and Mingo Counties, saw him at miners' meetings. By this time, having begun to sense his power with the voters, his opponents had begun to call him a Communist, a Socialist, an atheist.

"See, he don't believe in God," they cried.

"I'm not running against God," he replied.

He did it smiling. He did everything smiling. He is a smiling young man. When he was in the State Legislature, I saw, as any man sitting and watching could see, that his power in the State was due largely to knowledge. Young Holt had simply been a lamp-burner, a student. He had come from a race of men who were all students and he was running true to form. It was said of him, by newspaper men, and by other members of the State Legislature, when he was in Charleston as a member of the lower House—he jumped directly from that to the Democratic nomination for the United States Senate—"He knows more about the laws of this State, what they are, what they mean, how they got on the books, who put them on the books, than any man we have ever had in the House."

It was a year ago that I sat in the West Virginia State House, the Legislature being in session, watching him at work. Other members of the House kept running to him. "What does this bill mean? Explain it to me."

He did explain. When the House wasn't in session, he got into his car and, running over the State, explained to the voters. He went into a hundred county seat towns, explaining and explaining. As every one knows, most members of most State Legislatures are of a certain type. They are country lawyers. They do not get down to the State capitol very often. When they go down, as House members or as members of the State Senate, there is always a lot going on.

Almost every night a party—this lobbyist or that

lobbyist pulling a party. "Come on, boys. How about a little fun tonight?" A man doesn't have much time to get up on what is going on.

It takes a crank for that, a worker. It takes a man who wants to know.

And young Holt is that. I have watched him in the Legislature of his State. I have talked about him to young men and old men, merchants of his State and workers.

He speaks to the voters of the complaint that he is too young.

"I can't help that," he says. "I got born as soon as I could."

Rush Holt, the youngster, made his campaign for the Senatorship from West Virginia on facts. He is a fact hound. All of his speeches are an array of facts piled up. "Here is what my opponent says to you. Well, here is how he has voted." Not often needing written records, he has it all at his mind's edge, the exact time and place of every vote of every member of his State Legislature, not only in his own time but far back of that. He has the records of the Congressmen of his State, the Senators of his State. He told them, when he first went down to Charleston, as a young legislator, that he was going to do a lot of talking, and he has done a lot. He has come very near talking the

State of West Virginia into something new, something it never was before, a State curiously aware.

Rush Holt has made it that, and he isn't a crank or a fly-by-night. If he goes to Washington to represent his State in the Senate and he will—he won't go as the young McClellan went after certain West Virginia victories to the Army of the Potomac —as a young Napoleon. He will go as a fighting young student, a very smiling and warm young man. They feel now, over in West Virginia, that they have got, in their young Holt, something pretty good and significant in American politics. If young Holt keeps his head, and I fancy he will —if he goes on as he has begun, he will be too busy, as a student, to get the big head—if he goes on as he has begun, the whole country will presently be liking and admiring him as he is now liked and admired in West Virginia.

In the Middlewest

Revolt in South Dakota

Revolt in South Dakota

THE American woman, Gertrude Stein, who had been out of America for twenty-five or thirty years, living all of those years in Paris, had come back. She had been going about America—having a look—sometimes in a car, sometimes in a train, again by plane. She wanted to talk. She was excited.

"But you should have a year, two years, five years, just to begin to see it," I said. I didn't think she could get much of us, understand much, in a few weeks of flying about.

Right away, however, she said something. "Even when you are in a plane," she said, "you can tell when you pass out of one State and into another." She thought it was true, that there was always a sharp difference. "Now you are in Missouri. You pass on into Iowa or fly over Ohio.

"There is something in the way in which the farm buildings are grouped, in the way the towns are built, in something you feel in the people in the towns."

Miss Stein, by her talk, set me thinking of a kind of individuality I had myself seen and felt in the States.

For example, there is South Dakota. I had come down out of Minnesota, had taken a look at North Dakota. Was it true, as Miss Stein said, that I should be able to tell, even before I began talking with people, going to meetings, going into churches and stores, when I had come into a quite different State?

Almost at once I did feel a sharp difference. If North Dakota is the most radical of the States up in the Northwest section of the Middlewest, South Dakota is surely the most conservative.

And why? To be sure the State went for Roosevelt this year, but for many years States to the south of it, Nebraska and Kansas being, to say the least, sometimes politically experimental, North Dakota and Minnesota being pretty definitely and permanently radical, why did South Dakota begin by being conservative and remain so?

It is a self-conscious State, much more so I thought than Minnesota or North Dakota. At least in the other States people did not keep asking me the question, "What do they think of us back East? Are they interested? Are you going to write, boosting our State?" The country newspaper man, over the border in Minnesota—I won't put down the name of his town—some of the patriots of South Dakota might go over the border and get him—he told me— "It's a State that never should have been settled," he said.

It was his notion that the buffalo grass that used to grow out on the wide, wind-swept plains would have held the country down. "Now, it may all blow away," he said. "They have got this notion of dry farming in their heads. It's dry all right," he said. I walked with the country newspaperman about the streets of the frozen little town while he told me of the dust storms that came out of South Dakota, out of the plains beyond the Missouri, making the skies black at midday.

"Why," said the newspaperman, "I have an uncle who took up a farm out there.

"It was a farm until he plowed it," he said. "Then it blew away." By his story the uncle went about over his fields, picking up Indian arrow heads that had been buried a foot under ground. "The dry soil that had been plowed had drifted like drifting snow," he said. "He had planted trees and they were all killed. The fences were buried under the dust drifts.

"And if it isn't a dry season there are the grasshoppers to eat you up," he said. I got a blueenough picture from him.

You go into South Dakota having some such picture in your mind and what you find is disconcerting. I went to a meeting of the men's club at a church in a South Dakota town. All day I had been driving. Although I had been for days in heavy snows there was little or no snow on the plains.

It is true I had been seeing the sand-and-dust drifts, against the fences, trees killed by the drought, great patches of the trees' bark dropped off—there are no native trees—about each white farmhouse, sitting out on the long rolling plains, some farmer had planted trees about his house to serve as a wind break——

—Now, in great sections of the State, the trees are all killed—man's eternal and so often tragic war with nature—his struggle to command and control—out on the plains it is all there, to be seen, in the raw.

You see all this, noting the desolation brought by the drought, expecting to find a desolated and downtrodden people mourning in the streets, and then you go into one of the towns. There is a surprise for you. The people do all seem to be wearing last year's clothes and driving cars, plenty of them groaning, sputtering Model T Fords, but there is an air of cheerfulness. Right out in the heart of the drought country I saw towns, far from any pine trees, all festooned with green for the holidays. The men at the men's meeting at the church were cheerful fellows. They didn't seem too much discouraged. I could have seen many sadder-looking, more beaten men in any industrial town of the East. At the men's meeting in the church there was an effort made to raise money. A number of boys and girls from the country had been invited to a young people's meeting to be held in the town. There would be a certain expense. They were to stay but one day. It would cost fifty cents to feed a boy or a girl. "Who is willing to do it?" asked a man who had got to his feet. A merchant got up. "It isn't the money," he said. He thought a scheme ought to be worked out. "They should be made to feel they have earned it," he said. He thought it would be better for them. "But what, in Heaven's name are they to do?" some one asked. "I don't know," said the merchant.

I found a man at the men's meeting who wanted to talk. You always find them.

And so we went from the church to his house.

He also had got it into his head that I might be writing something about South Dakota and was afraid I wouldn't be fair. The man had five or six big ears of corn lying on the mantel in the living room of his house. "I can't offer you anything to drink," he said apologetically. "We're a dry State yet.

"I mean about liquor," he added quickly. He seemed afraid that if I did write I would over-emphasize the drought, its consequences to the State, etc. He had a cousin who owned a farm in the Sioux River Valley, over near the Iowa line. He took one of the big ears and broke it into two pieces, demanding that I note how closely and firmly the grains of corn were set together. "It's from my brother's farm, right here in South Dakota and was raised this year," he said proudly. I had found this feeling everywhere, a kind of touchiness, as though, to these people of South Dakota, the land on which they lived was like a child that misbehaved sometimes—as for example the drought that could not be concealed—but that was nevertheless their child. "Be careful how you speak of it," they all seemed to be saying.

The man in whose house I sat began telling me —his voice full of resentment—of a writer from one of the big Eastern magazines who had come out during the drought. "The dirty cuss," he said vehemently. "I hate such men," he added. The writer had come into the land in the terrifically hot, dry summer and had seen and written of cattle dying and lying in fence corners, had been in sections of the State to which water had to be hauled by train, had been in one of the dust storms, the sky black with dust, top soil of thousands of acres blowing away, no cars running in the roads, men and women huddled in their houses, the street lights in towns lighted at noonday. "Man, what do you expect?" I asked. I tried to explain to him about us writers. "That sort of thing is just meat and drink for one of us.

"If not to find in all of this something terrible or strange and then to play up the terrible and strange, why do you suppose an Eastern magazine would send one of us out here?" I tried to explain to him how I had myself come into the State with my mind already half made up. For one thing I had been reading a novel, written out of the dry country—and a very good one, too—the bitterness of men and women on farms, seeing the crops slowly shrivel up, the ponds and wells go dry, a kind of insanity coming over the people.

"Yes, I know," the man said. He made a queer twisted movement with his lips. "Do you know what we did? We went to church and knelt down. It seemed to me we were like fools there, on our knees, Sunday after Sunday, praying for rain, and no rain coming at all.

"I guess if God wants to send rain he doesn't

have to ask us," the man added, and when I left his house, to step out into the biting cold of the night—his house was at the very edge of his town —it was a moonlit night—he had come after me, bare-headed out of the house, and as we stood in the yard we could see for miles out over the South Dakota plains—there were farmhouses with big red barns out there, the cribs and barns empty now, they stuck up out of the land like sore thumbs that night, the trees so carefully planted and tended about the houses all dead now. The man still had something on his mind. "On the whole," he said, "I think we'd rather you writers let us alone." He got bitter.

"If you are going to write, saying ours is a no-good country, why not write in the same way about parts of Iowa and North Dakota?

"And Nebraska, too?

"Or better than that, why not come here in a good year?"

The man turned and walked away from me, back into the house, slamming his door. He was like many others I saw, very determined about the real worth to man, as a place to live, of his State.

As for the long and persistent dryness of the drought I myself saw something. There was a little white church sitting beside a road out in a great flat place. There was not a tree in sight. "It would be here they came to pray for the rain," I thought. This was in a very dry section of the State. That day I had seen places where the sand and dust drifts had all but covered the fences, had seen the corn in cornfields, cut and shocked, the shocks far apart, standing up hardly higher than my knees. I stopped the car and getting out went to walk around the church, thinking, as I did so, of what the man in the house had told me.

Thinking also of what I had seen. As when I had driven down out of the hills of southwestern Virginia, Kentucky, and Tennessee into Ohio, Illinois, and Indiana I had been struck by the opulence and magnificence of the farmhouses and outbuildings, so again in South Dakota. "In these other States, that is to say in Ohio, Indiana, and Illinois, there would at least have been forests," I told myself. In South Dakota they would have had to bring in the timber for all of the buildings, hauling it for hundreds of miles. "It would have cost like the Old Harry," I thought. "These people are right to be proud of what their land can do in a good year."

I walked around the country church. It was a week day and the church was closed. It didn't matter. The long dry year just passed had done its work well. It had curled up the boards covering the sides of the building so that you could look through and see the daylight streaming in from the opposite side, that certainly making a picture in the mind to be remembered, of people coming there, to worship, in the midst of the drought the sun-burned people, men and women——

You have to think of them as coming from distant farmhouses, past their own fields, where the corn is shrivelled away to nothingness, the fields their own hands have plowed, planted, and tended, only to see the crops all burn away to a dry ash of dust.

Then kneeling down in the church to pray, the very boards of the church cracking and curling under the dry heat, the paint on the boards frying in the hot winds, perhaps a breeze blowing, and the dust of the fields sifting in through the cracks. Dust in the mouths of the people as they prayed for the rain.

It may all be a matter of the land . . . the land men all, or nearly all, naturally conservative. The South Dakota newspaperman with whom I talked late into a cold night thought it was so. There are practically no industries in the State. In the far West, in the Black Hills, there is a gold mine out of which millions have been taken. They are still taking it, and the farmers would like to grab the mine. They would like to make it lift the load of taxes off of the land. More than a third of the people of the State, the farmers and the town people, are now on relief.

I went up into a little interior town. It was still very cold. Deep snow in Iowa and in Minnesota but none here. In the town they had been praying for the snow. It would put moisture back into the baked-out ground, help with next year's crop. In an Eastern magazine I had read an article, written so I had heard by a man of the town, an article full of the promise of revolt, and in a little country print shop I found two old men.

The print shop was very small. There was a small stove, and an old man came to sit with me. He was a gentle-faced old man with snow-white hair. We spoke of automobiles, and he told me that he owned a Ford. "It is a Model T," he said. "I bought it for twenty-five dollars." He said he had driven the Ford some twenty-five thousand miles. The old man had a passion. "I go to some print shop, like this," he said. "I work there. In my spare time I print little books.

"I am going to organize a new party," he said. He laughed softly, telling me of a convention he had called. I gathered that he had some plan for a new handling of the monetary question. "I named a town where we would hold the convention and drove there in my Ford." I gathered that this was during the summer when the whole country was burned dry, when the corn in the fields was going dead in the dry winds. I imagined him going along the road, meeting on the way men and women who were hauling water, perhaps from the Missouri River, hauling it across the plains, the sky overhead gray with the floating dust. The little old man had already given me one of his booklets to read, the booklets half the size of an ordinary envelope and printed on cheap newsprint, some eight small pages in each booklet. He had written a number of little childlike stories, each story to illustrate some phase of what would happen to society if his plan were adopted. Afterwards I saw the old man at a big Farmers Union meeting, a meeting to which I went filled with hope. I wanted a real story and had been told, it had been intimated to me, that at the meeting some of the orators among the farmers would break forth. I was to hear things that would startle me but nothing of the sort happened at all. Although I saw many destitute-looking farmers at the meeting, heard stories enough of men who a few years before were prosperous men and were now on relief, the meeting was very quiet, very orderly. There was a young high school girl who got up and sang, rather badly I thought. The mayor of the town made a speech. He was a man of fifty and boasted that he had never been out of his State. "I was born here. I am still here," he declared proudly. Several country boys, a small-town orchestra, played a piece on guitars and banjos. A big farmer leaned over and whispered to me. "They've been on the radio," he said. The meeting was much like some of the meetings of Kiwanis I attended a few years ago, when I was active in running my country newspapers in Virginia.

But there was my gentle little old man of the pamphlets. He was going about. He was distributing his booklets. He came and whispered to me. "I am stirring up a lot of interest here," he said. On that other day, when I was visiting the little print shop, where he was employed temporarily and where he had talked to me at length, trying to make me understand his plan for the new party based on a new handling of our monetary system, that would save the agricultural West, his battered but still serviceable Ford standing in a vacant lot back of the shop, on that occasion I had been very insistent on the article I had read in the magazine.

As I have suggested there were two old men in the shop. The second man was setting up an advertisement. He was tall and silent but was also a sweet-faced man. "So there was this article," I said. "I am looking for signs of revolt.

"After all I am also a writer. I have come out here. If there is revolt here I would like to know of it. Who are the leaders? What's going on?" I asked. I had it in my mind that the article in question had been written by a native of the little town out on the plains. It had been quite specific. "In a few months, at most in a year or two, revolt would come." That was about the tone of what I had read. The tall old man, who was setting up the advertisement of a January white sale for the town's general store, came to stand by the stove. Both of the old men laughed. The smaller of the two men rubbed his hands together.

"That was like the convention I called for my new party," he said. "You see I went to the town where the convention was to be held in my Ford. I drove a long ways. There was a dust storm and I had to stay overnight in a barn.

"I was the only one who came," he said giggling.

He and the tall old man seemed deeply amused. "As for that article you read in that magazine," the tall man said, the article about the revolt coming in South Dakota"—(the whole thing must have been a standing joke between the two). "These Eastern fellows, writers, who come out here—" he looked at the small man and winked. "No," he said, "it wasn't written by any one in this town.

"There was an Eastern fellow, like you," he said. "He came out here. He was here for a while. He went about speaking to people as you are now doing. He was a lucky one," he said.

"Do you know what," said the smaller of the two men, leaning over the stove. His eyes were shining. "Do you know what?

"He sold the article he had written for a hundred and seventy-five dollars. Think of the booklets I could print and distribute for all of that money," said the little old man. "I could get my new party started at last."

He had stopped smiling. I thought there was a hungry look in his eyes and in the eyes of the tall one as well.

When Relief Relieves

Village Wassail

THE little Middlewestern city has lived through two stirring periods. The first goes far back to when white men first came crowding into the country. That was when the Northern pine woods still stood. I saw and talked with a hardy little old man of ninety. He can still sit reading his newspaper without glasses and was glad to talk of the deep woods—how all winter the great logs trundled down into the frozen river, and of the big spring drive. There were five or six big band mills at the head of river navigation, every other door a saloon, booted lumberjacks coming down for holidays out of the woods, the gambling houses going full tilt.

A stirring life, men being made rich, plenty of work for the common man, money to spend, and then suddenly it was all at an end, and the forests were gone.

The life of the city fell away. It became a dead place, and then came a second boom. "You would never have thought, if you had been with us in the pine woods, the trees standing so thick you could hardly push your way through, that it would ever become a rich farming country," the old lumberjack said.

It did become a rich farming country, and then came the railroads and factories. A new life, the factory hands in town and the farm life out there beyond the river to the West and along the railroads to the North, East, and South. There was a little town every ten or twelve miles on each of the three railroads, wholesale houses in the city, travelling men going out.

Good times. Good times. The farmers with their big houses and big barns, the wholesalers in town, the factory owners, even the factory hands, all became Republicans. There were big majorities thrown up for the McKinleys, the Hardings, the Coolidges. Prohibition came with the World War. "They did a lot of drinking just the same," the little doctor I had got in with, told me. He explained that it was mostly the youngsters, fellows come home from the war, the young women of that time, the far-famed "lost generation." The doctor said that the drinking and the so-called fun didn't touch most of the people. There was a kind of war, an undercurrent of feeling between town and country. "There was too much grabbing and politics was out," the doctor said. The doctor was one of a good many men I have met who didn't too much regret the boom years. The racketeers were flourishing and the people had given up looking to government for help. "We thought government was a racket too, that it had to be a racket," the doctor said.

I was very curious about something I had noticed all over the Middlewest and so I went with the doctor and a friend of his to a certain place. We went on a rainy November night. "Are there such places at the outer edge of your city?" I had asked the doctor, and, "Yes, plenty of them, I'll take you," he had answered. He got his friend, the newspaper publisher, and we went in the doctor's car out of the Northwestern city and over a long bridge and into a suburban factory district. We went through that and up a hill to a beer-selling place on a hill, to where the farms began.

As we drove out I was thinking of the city and of the several days spent tramping around in it and talking to men. There was a big shoe factory, a foundry, an overall factory, factories where clothing was made, and several woodworking plants. For a time they had all been closed. Some of them are again running on part time now.

I had driven up into the city from the South-east, and it had been all of a long day's drive in a rich farming country. In spite of the long depression there had been the big barns and houses, the herds of fine-looking cattle in barnyards, the corn standing shocked in the fields. I was at the edge of the drought country, but here the corn had come through. I could tell this by the size of the shocks still in the fields, the full cribs, the golden yellow Middlewestern corn showing through the slats of the cribs. I had even stopped the car and had gone into barnyards to have a look. There were the long fat ears, filled to the tips with the grains, the famous Middlewestern corn.

—Tales enough of farmers in debt, being sold up, penny sales, tenants thrown off farms, strikes of farmers, angry countrymen gathered at crossroads with shotguns in hand——

I went with the two men, the doctor and the newspaper publisher, up a muddy road to the hill at the edge of the far Northern city. I had asked them to take me to some such place because my curiosity had been aroused. I had noticed that such places were springing up everywhere, all over the Middlewest, always at the edges of towns, where town met country. Country editors and others, men I had formerly known, had spoken to me of them. I had got a feeling that they were something new in American drinking places—not at all like the old saloons I had known in my boyhood in the Middlewest—I wanted to know.

I was in such a place with the two men with whom I had scratched up an acquaintance, and it was a dismal, rainy November night, and in the place I saw broad-shouldered, big-handed farmers, who came in cars that were often old and rickety—and they came bringing their wives. They drove up, rubbing mud off their boots at the door, and came into the hot, smoky little room to join the others, already there, town people a part of them—most of them were known to my acquaintance, the doctor—they were mechanics of the industrial suburb out of work, factory hands on part time, men and women without work and on relief. There were others—a small-time prizefighter unable to get engagements now, a man who had been athletic director of the Y. M. C. A. in the city, and more and more farmers.

They had all come, bringing their wives. That was to me, oddly enough, the amazing thing. I had travelled a good deal in America in the past, had been in all kinds of places, in a good many drinking places.

But was it first of all a drinking place? I wondered. It seemed to be rather a new kind of meeting place. There was no heavy drinking. I saw no drunkenness. There was the room, such as might once have been a country store, with a bar in one corner and tables along a wall. The doctor, the newspaper publisher, and I sat in a corner. There was a piano in another corner, and a place in the centre of the room had been left free for dancing.

We had gone in there and the doctor had begun to talk of the people in the room and right away the other man, the newspaper publisher, began trying to refute everything the doctor said. There was a curious kind of relationship between the two men—a thing often met with among American men in the smaller towns and cities. There are two men, who stick to each other, who are friends, but who never by any chance agree. When one has made a statement the other is bound to challenge. It is a kind of ritual of the friendship, and it had already come out in these two men. They had quarrelled all the way over to the place, and when we got there they continued to quarrel.

"These people," said the doctor—"there is a man over there—" He pointed to the prizefighter. He wanted to tell me of something he felt about the people in the room, of a kind of sympathetic interest he felt in them, but the newspaper publisher kept interrupting. He kept condemning the people in the little beer hall, declaring that most of them were of no account. "I'm an individualist," he said. "You must not listen to the doc here, he's a sentimentalist." He began saying that more than half the people in the room were on relief. "This room is half full of them," he said. "The government is ruining the people. Here are these people. They are drinking and dancing— most of them getting money from the government with which to do it. They will never work any more. They will not want to work."

The newspaper publisher kept grumbling, but the doctor went on with the story he had begun. "Oh, you!" he said, making a contemptuous movement with his hand toward the doctor. The newspaper publisher was big and fat, and the doctor was a small alert man. He had a little gray mustache.

The doctor told a story of the prizefighter who sat with his wife, a pretty little black-haired woman, at a nearby table.

Some days before the pair had gotten into a quarrel. "Well, you see," said the doctor, "he didn't intend to do it, but he is in the habit of using his fists. He struck out. They had this quarrel, and he rapped her one. He blackened her eye."

The prizefighter's wife had formerly been, I gathered, something of a figure in the city. Her father had been a well-to-do man, and then, in that famous year, in twenty-nine, when so many others went down, down he went. They were down and out, and she, the daughter, who might have been a society dame, had seen the young prizefighter and had fallen for him. So she went off and married the man. "Why not?" said the doctor.

He thought it had been all right, but the prizefighter also was without money. He could not get any engagements and they had to live in two cramped rooms in a laborer's house, so they got into a quarrel and during the quarrel the doctor said he popped her one.

"And then he came to my office. He was scared. He was crying like a kid and going on, so I got him in my car and we went out to where they were living. She was all right," the doctor declared, describing his interview with the woman. "After all, what harm in a black eye?" He had gone to where the two lived and there was the little black-haired woman grinning. "It was my fault. He did just right," she told the doctor. She took all of the blame on herself because she said she had been bellyaching. "I was speaking out of my turn," she told the doctor. "It's no time for bellyachers now."

The doctor told his story of the two town people in the room, and the newspaperman kept scoffing at him. There was a little outbreak of quarrelling between the two. It concerned the farmers. It was true, the newspaper publisher said, that a good many of the town workers couldn't get any work. Most of the factories had been closed. "But these farmers," he said. "The farmers," he declared, "had always been the champion bellyachers." The newspaperman had got a good start and he kept going. I could see that he was trying to irritate the doctor, who kept pulling at his mustache and looking about the room. He said that it had been proposed in some of the States that people on relief be deprived of their vote. He was for that. "A pauper is a pauper," he said, winking at me. He began on the subject of man and his opportunities. "I don't care what comes up, the man who has got the'real stuff in him will survive. He will get to the front." He said that he thought that it was a crying shame that men who were on relief should come with their wives at night to such places as the one we were in. "Here they are," he said, "dancing. They have even brought their wives. They might better be out looking for jobs." "What, tonight," the doctor asked, "in the rain?"

The two men kept at their little quarrel. I had been with them on two other occasions and had grown used to it. Sometimes we were in the doctor's car and sometimes in my own, or in the newspaperman's car. When one of the two men did the driving the other constantly criticized. "You are a doctor. You make most of your living taking care of nervous old women. You have become a nervous old woman yourself," the newspaperman said, growling at his friend. The newspaperman had come into the Northwest out of the East. In the boom year of 'twenty-eight he had bought the daily newspaper there. "I'm broke," he had told me that afternoon. He declared in the presence of the doctor that he was against everything that was going on in the government, but most of all he was against relief. In the place to which he had come, on that November night, he kept growling at the people, some of them sitting at the tables along the wall, others dancing, and the doctor had gone into a contemptuous silence.

I was looking about the room. Already I had gone alone into several such places and they had all been pretty much alike. There was the same mixture of town and country people, and in all of the places I had visited I had been struck by the predominance of middle-aged couples.

There would be, in each place, the piano in one corner and a young girl playing it. The girl at the piano that night was a little thin thing with thin arms and a thin voice. She kept thumping bravely away and occasionally broke into a thin song. A workman, a rather sturdy-looking man of forty, in overalls, got out on the floor and began to do a jig. His wife, a strong-looking woman also of forty—I thought she looked curiously like the American Parisian, Gertrude Stein—was leaning forward in her chair and watching, and when the man had finished his solo performance and had returned to her, I saw her lean over and pat him on the back. She whispered something to him and they both began to laugh.

And now most of the people in the room had begun to dance, and the doctor left us and went to dance with one of the women. The newspaper-man told me that she was the wife of a man who had formerly owned a garage. "It's closed now," he said. We were alone together and the newspaperman became contrite. He already knew what I was doing, that I was going about and looking at people. "This fellow may be writing of things he has seen and has heard people say," he thought. He began to tell me that I must not take seriously the things he had said in the presence of the doctor.

I was to notice, he said, how little real drinking there was in the room, and he began to explain to me what I had already noticed. "These people come here, into these places," he said. Such places were springing up near all of the towns. There had been a heavy gloom lying over the towns and over the nearby farms. "If you've got any stuff in you, you can stay in that state of gloom about so long, and then—well you either commit suicide or you throw it off." Many of the men I saw that night in the dance hall had formerly been fairly prosperous men. The town men had been of the sort who had bought and often partly paid for their homes, and now they were broke. "If the banks should close down on me I would be in the same position they are," the newspaperman declared. He thought I should go into more of the people's homes. "You go with the doc, you stick to him, get him to take you," he said. He seemed anxious to reassure me concerning his friend.

He said again that a good many of the men in the room that night had once owned or had partly paid for comfortable homes that were now lost. Such a one might now be living with his wife and often with children, in two or three crowded, un-comfortable rooms in the town. He then told me something I had already sensed.—"In my news-paper," he said, "as in my talk with the doc, I say a lot of things I don't really believe." As for the people in the little dance hall, it was quite true that many of them were on relief.—"What are they going to do?" he asked. There was a serious problem up—the most serious the American peo-ple had ever faced. "But what," he said, "was the use of meeting it with long faces?"—There would be such a man and his wife. Let us say that the fellow and his wife had several children. Often an arrangement had been made with a neighbor. Mrs. Jones and her man would take care of Mrs. Smith's children tonight and tomorrow night it would be the turn of Mr. and Mrs. Smith. "And so they come here, or to some such place," he said. He thought it was a new development in Ameri-can life. At least it was so in the Middlewest. He had been to Europe several times when he was a young man, and there the people had long ago learned something the Americans were just be-ginning to learn. "They have learned that it doesn't cost so much to have a fairly good time. The problem for the people to face is to get at each other. The town and the country have to get together." He said that he thought that half of the affection of the people for the Roosevelts, man and wife—at least it was so in the Middle-west—was due to the fact that the Roosevelts didn't surrender to gloom.

"Good Heavens," said the newspaperman, "there are people who are bellyaching about relief." He laughed. "I do it myself when I am with the doc," he said. "But tomorrow I may myself be on relief," he added. He was busy putting himself right with me about the dancing couples in the room, the middle-aged Americans, men with their wives, out for the evening, spending perhaps twenty to thirty cents during the evening—the little thin Middlewestern American girl thump-ing away at the piano—getting let's say a dollar for the night—this going on in thousands of such little places all over the Middlewest—the grim pathos of it—a slow growing understanding be-tween town and country growing up just the same —the gameness of the people coming out——

I went from the dance hall back to my hotel with the two men, the newspaperman having got back into the mood of ragging his friend the doc-tor—declaring again that the relief program of the government was ruining the people. "You get any one of this crowd on relief and you'll never get him off," he declared.

The newspaperman again kept talking in this way, ragging his friend, the doctor— I had got into my room at the hotel and had settled myself for the night when the doctor knocked on my door. He was concerned about something. He was like the newspaperman. He was very anxious that I not misunderstand his friend. He did not come into the room but stood at the door. He was nervous. He wanted me to know that at bottom the newspaperman and he were really in agreement. "That is," he said, "just the point." He very much wanted me to understand that he and his friend were really friends, that they felt alike. He did not want me to get either one of them wrong. "I just want you to know," he said. He hesitated, finding it a little hard to say what he wanted to say. "It's about these people on relief," he said, standing at my hotel door late that night. I could see that he was afraid, having seen the people in the little beer hall, dancing there, even some of them spending a little of the relief money to buy a little pleasure, the middle-aged men who had once been prosperous bringing their wives to the place—he was terribly afraid that I would go puritanic, would write something in the tone of the newspaperman when he was ragging his friend. He had been unable to go home and to bed thinking about it, and now he stood at my hotel-room door.—"I hope I didn't get you out of bed, I wanted to be sure you knew that Jim feels as I do," he said. (Jim was the name of the newspaperman.) We want you to know that we both feel that relief isn't relief if it takes the guts out of them," he said, and I thought he had the air of one pleading with me.

Night in a Corn Town

Night in a Corn Town

IT was a cold November day with flurries of snow. A kindly farmer having picked me up brought me down to a garage, in a little Ohio town, my car having gone back on me. A man in overalls went from the garage to get my car. I had been trying to get the feel of the country. "Why not begin here?" I thought. "I am presumed to be reporting the lives of ordinary American men in these times." This was my own Middlewest, where I had not been for ten years.

Well, yes, I had. Some five or six years before I was in some of the cities of Ohio delivering literary lectures. "Thank Heavens I am not doing that now." I went, that time, to the big industrial centres. We literary fellows have our weaknesses. If we have written books we like to go among people who have heard of us. We get into little groups, having the same interest as our own. We pat each other on the back. Nowdays most of us literary fellows have an inclination to be on the radical side. We are, as you might say, leftward. Just before I left home a writer came to see me.

He had been in a Middlewestern city where there had been a strike. He is a very serious-minded man and told me about the Middlewestern farmers and the people in the smaller Middlewestern towns. "They are ready for anything," he said. "Revolution is coming."

I didn't believe that so I went to a church—this in a small town—and there the minister was telling his people about New York City. He hadn't been in New York but some one had told him, "New York is ready for almost anything," he said. Oh, the great wicked city! He might have been speaking of Prague or of Pekin. How far away and foreign seemed the city he described to his congregation. I had just come from the city. He described a parade of radicals through the streets. "They marched five abreast. It took them all day to pass a given point." He said there were two hundred and fifty thousand of them. "Whew," I thought. "They carried banners inscribed, 'Down with God,' 'Down with Government.'" I was glad enough to escape from both the minister and my friend the radical, from the man who talked of New York, not having been in New York, and from the city man who spoke of the farms and of the small towns.

"I would like the feel of things. What's going

on?" I had been thinking. Is there a slow and groping feeling toward the left? In country garages and drug stores in the little Middlewestern towns you will hear serious talk of old age pensions, of unemployment insurance. The election just past had a curious angle. They do not say that such and such a man carried Indiana, Ohio, or Iowa. They say Roosevelt carried the States. The minds of the people are fixed upon Roosevelt. Their hopes are in him.

"If we could get away from the fear of dying poor, in the poorhouse." "It isn't my fault if I can't get work. I want it. I want it."

Anything like revolution means to the American mind just the one thing. There is the picture of men standing, with their backs to a wall, in the act of being shot. Your average American doesn't think of himself as being one of those who are doing the shooting. "It would be just my luck to be one of those standing there, with my back to the wall."

There is a slow shifting of loyalty among the Negroes. In the Middlewest they vote. They have been drifting away from the Republican Party. "For a long time," one of them said to me, "we stuck, hoping maybe we'd help our brothers down South.

"We can't see that they've ever been helped much."

Is there a new feeling about property, something slowly getting into men's minds through the long depression? I am writing out of the little towns and the farms, have not been, at this moment, as I sit writing these words, much in the industrial centres.

There are men out now husking corn, in November fields. Men are coming into the little towns, to court and to the stores. The hunting season will soon open. Even the man out of work and now that the election is over, no more political meetings to go to—"anyway I like to hear them cuss each other"—now they are getting out guns. Bill, out of work and broke, will borrow a gun from Jim. He'll get Fred's dog for a day.

I had got into the land of the long cornfields, in central Ohio. "This," I thought, "is much like the Illinois and Iowa corn lands I have known in the past." The garage, where I waited for my car to be hauled in and put back in running shape again, was just off the main street. From the back of the garage you could look out, past small frame houses, into the fields. Here, in this Ohio country, they do not strip the corn, as they do farther south, in Kentucky and Tennessee, nor as they do farther west, husk it as it stands in the field, the teams and wagons working their way through the standing corn—bang of the big yellow ears against bang boards—that making a kind of corn music, too. Here they cut the corn and stand it in shocks. It may be that I got a little poetic, standing in the small Ohio town garage, listening to the talk, looking out at the back toward the fields.

The corn, in its shocks, standing up like armies of soldiers in the fields. "There are these armies out there," I was saying to myself. There were old battle pictures I had seen. The central Ohio country is a land of low hills. From one low hill to the next there is a long sweep, perhaps ten miles across. When the leaves are off the trees in the fall you can see from one town to the next. In the old battle pictures, Napoleon at Austerlitz, Meade at Gettysburg, you saw regiments marching massed across just such fields. "And there are these armies here, the corn standing shocked in the fields. With all these long cornfields of the Middlewest man will surely eat.

"With these armies, standing at attention out there, we will be ready to fight the grim shadowy armies of want."

Myself going on in this way, standing in the

garage. Other men were waiting there, men were loafing there. My car had been brought in. There was a stoppage in the gas feed line. I was glad that I hadn't again forgotten to put in gas. There was still some in the tank. I am always forgetting, thinking a car will run on gasless forever.

Myself, that day, with a kind of nostalgia for the land. In an Ohio town passed through that day, I had spent a part of my boyhood. We lived at the edge of the town, in an old rented frame house, the cornfields coming down to our kitchen door.

There was the grand cycle of the corn. How much in America it has meant! When the pioneers came into the country the thing to be done was to clear a little piece for the corn.

The fields getting bigger and bigger, the stumps rooted out.

The preparing of the land in the spring, the corn planting. Memories of boyhood days, wandering with other boys in the tall corn, in July and August. It grew high above our heads.

How strange and mysterious it was. Why has not more of our American song been concerned with the corn? You could get lost in the tall corn. Once a younger brother was lost at night in a cornfield near our house. Neighbors were going through the corn with lanterns. There were cries. Voices called. There was the flash of lanterns at night in the forests of the corn.

And then, in the daytime a boy often alone, venturing in, under the corn and along the rows. You could lie in there, on the warm ground. There was the little life of insects in the ground, the soft green light sifting down through the thick corn leaves, a little wind blowing and the yellow pollen of the corn falling down in your hair. Faraway, under the corn, you saw a rabbit hopping leisurely along.

I cannot tell how much of all this, set down above—I had been caught up with a curiously warm feeling of home-coming all that day—this in spite of the November day, a chill wind blowing, gray clouds covering the Ohio skies—how much of all this did I say to the tall farmer who presently came up to me. He spoke to me. He was the man who had picked me up in the road and he had seen the Virginia license on my car. "It's getting late in the day stranger," he said. He spoke of the little hotel in the town. "It isn't so much. There may be rain." As it turned out the skies cleared and it grew warmer during the evening. "I'd be pleased to have you come home with me for the night."

It is possible that at the farmer's table I talked some more of the nonsense that was in my head. Is it nonsense? I began to go on about the cornfields, how they made me feel, my pleasure in getting back to the tall corn, to the land of the big cornfields. I described the cornfields of our Virginia, Tennessee, and Kentucky hills, the little fields clinging to the sides of the hills. "Some day the government will make men quit plowing such fields," I said. "The hills will be put back into forests. The rains are carrying all the good ground away."

"But," I said, "there are men there who are devoted to their poor little fields. The government will have to take care of them."

I must have gone back to my talk of the armies of the corn, using, I dare say, some rather highfalutin' language. The farmer, a tall old man with a gray mustache, his rather fat wife, and the daughter—she was young yet but she would be a handsome woman—they sat listening in silence. It had grown warmer at the end of the day and, after eating, I was shown out to the front porch of the house. The house was at the end of a street and at the edge of the town and beyond the fields began. "It has got warm. Let's sit out here for a while," said the farmer, and leaving me he went into the house.

It was quiet on the porch and there were chairs. Inside the house I heard the farmer at the phone. "Come on over here," I heard him say. He let his voice drop, not wanting me to hear. "I've got something here," he said, and laughed. There was something self-conscious in his voice. "He means me. He thinks I am a nut," I told myself, but at the moment I did not much care.

On the porch, in the night, it was I thought very nice. A new moon had come up. Inside the house I could hear the rattling of dishes, but presently the sound ceased and I heard the farmer moving about. I heard his wife whisper to him. "Naw," he said. He came out to me. "She thinks maybe you are some kind of an agent," he said, making a motion with his head. He sat in a chair. "I've asked a man to come over here." I had a notion that the wife and the daughter were sitting and listening just inside the door. "They will be listening to hear what we say," I thought. The farmer began to explain about his position in life. It was an old story. He told me about the man he had asked to come to the house. "He's a tenant," he said.

He said the man had been living on a part of his farm but that there had been a misunderstanding. He leaned forward in his chair. "You are

247

a stranger," he said. He began to tell me about the position he was in. He had two hundred acres of land, he said, but had got into debt. "I cannot pay the interest," he said. He did not say so directly, but I gathered that he had something in his mind. It concerned the tenant on his land, the man he had asked to come to the house. "He has been trying to gouge the fellow," I thought. I jumped to that conclusion. "He is a little dissatisfied with the deal I am offering him for the next year. We have been together, working together for a long time, but now he is talking of trying some other place."

The tenant arrived. He was a short, heavily built man, and right away I saw that he was shy. I had given the farmer my name, and there was the awkward formality of an introduction but the tenant said nothing. He would not take a chair but sat at the edge of the porch with his back to a post.

There was a time of silence. "Well," I thought, "this will not do," and I began to talk. I began to make conversation. To tell the truth I began to lie. In the two men, sitting thus with me, I felt a strain. "The one man owns the land on which they have both worked, but these two men here have been something more to each other than employer and employee," I thought.

"They have been friends, working together on the same land, in the same fields but something has happened. It concerned money, the interest on a debt on the land." On the telephone the land owner had tried to speak in a friendly way to the tenant, but, face to face, the two men could not talk. There was the queer prolonged silence common to country people who have got into a quarrel.

I began to tell the story of a dream I had had, It was a lie. There was no such dream. "Why have an imagination if you cannot use it?" I thought. I was inventing as I talked. I told a story of my own little farm in the hills of Virginia.

And so, in the story I told and in my dream I was on my farm. It was night and I walked in fields. I was climbing the hills. "And there were the fields," I said. "They are poor enough fields but, in the dream, they had become persons to me." I had got started and I went on. "I am going good," I thought. The two men on the porch were very attentive. Something was thawing. I went on inventing. There were old-women fields and there were old-men fields.

249

"There were fields," I said, "that had become old maids.

"No man had ever plowed them," I said.

I went on with my fanciful tale. In the dream I was inventing I had come to a field far up the side of a hill, at the edge of the farm. "That," I said, "was the mother of all the fields on my farm."

In the dream I stood by a fence at the edge of the field and I said that the field whispered to me. "My richness has been drained away to the other fields," it said. The field had scolded me, as old women will.

I had got going and I went on, talking of the land and of how, in the night, in a dream, an old ruined field had whispered to me, but presently I was stopped by my host. "Yes," he said, "I get you," he said.

The Ohio farmer had got up out of his chair and had begun walking nervously up and down the length of the porch. "I've got him," I thought. The tenant, that short, broad-shouldered man, was also touched. I had awakened in him a personal feeling for the land on which he had worked. He had taken a knife out of his pocket and I saw him thrusting the blade into the boards of the porch.

And now my host, the Ohio farm owner, had also begun to talk. He began speaking of an experience he had had. "It was when I was a boy," he said. He told a tale of a drought in the land when he was a boy. "There has been a drought this year, further West, in some of the States, but the worst of it did not get to us," he said. He was not addressing his remarks to me but to that man, his tenant, sitting and listening. The tenant, who had been silent all evening, had got up and sat now in one of the chairs and the farmer stopped walking and stood with his back against one of the posts of the porch. "He is taking the man back into partnership," I thought.

There was a feeling of something between the two men that had been tense and now had become relaxed and when the farmer, standing with his back to the post, had finished his tale I excused myself, saying that I was sleepy, and went, led by the farmer's wife, upstairs to my room. The farmer had told the story of the drought in the land during his boyhood. His father, he said, had taken him one night, when the drought was at its worst, into the fields. "He talked as you have been talking," he said turning to me, "only that he spoke of the fields as his children.

"He spoke of them as children, having a fever,"

the farmer said, and then his tale came to an end. He had become embarrassed by his own words, and I excused myself. "I will go to bed now," I said, and, when he had called his fat wife, I went with her upstairs in the house and to my room.

I was feeling proud, and for a long time I lay awake. I could hear the two men talking on the porch below, and I heard the farmer's wife and the daughter preparing for bed in neighboring rooms. "I may not be the poet of the cornfields that I have been crying for all day," I thought, "but as a talker—an itinerant maker-up of tales of dreams of the land—I am pretty good." I could hear the sound of the movement of cattle among dry cornstalks in a nearby field. "They have broken out the corn in that field and have left the stalks standing," I thought. I fancied that they had turned some steers into the field. I went presently to sleep but afterwards awoke. The Ohio farmer, my host for the night, had come upstairs and was getting ready for bed. I heard him speak to his wife. "Well, Mother, I have fixed it with John," he said. "He is going to stay on our place."

Olsonville

Olsonville

THE Northwestern farm woman at the back of the hall at the political meeting watched anxiously the little girl who had been called up to draw the tickets in the turkey raffle. The tickets were ten cents each and she had three of them. It was a big turkey. The man on the platform said it weighed twenty-eight pounds. I watched the woman's big red hands as they gripped the tickets. She sat in a chair by the wall at the back of the hall and as the preparations for the drawing of the lucky number went forward I could see her eyes. They kept looking down at the tickets, noting the numbers, memorizing them. "Four hundred and sixty-three, and four, and five." Her lips moved and I was noting the big shoulders of the woman, the three- or four-year-old dress she wore, the big Swedish face and the general bigness and bonyness of her frame. I had seen the tall boy, of thirteen, in worn overalls, bring her the tickets and had thought, "That's the kind of stuff out of which a coach produces the University of Minnesota football teams.

"The Thundering Herd." Was that the name the sporting writers for the Minnesota dailies called it? I had seen the team play and had been thrilled. Oh, the power of it, the dancing rhythm, the quick co-ordination! What a gorgeous American game, and how American it is! The time for the drawing of the lucky number had come, and I saw the woman lean over and speak to another big woman, also a farm woman.

But wait. The second woman, also Scandinavian, might have been the wife of a town worker. The political meeting was being held in a Minnesota town and there were factories there. It was snowing outside, had been snowing steadily for three days, and I was marooned in the town. My little car could no longer buck the drifts. "I won't have any luck. I know I won't," the big woman said to her big woman neighbor. She was trying to cross up her luck, not to crowd it. I could see that. There was, in her eyes, an intense hunger to win that turkey. "She wants it. She sure needs it," I thought.

I had been going about, picking up stories of the political struggles of the last six, eight, ten years in the Northwest, of the struggles in Minnesota, North Dakota, South Dakota. It had been a little hard to keep on the political slant. "Well, then, let the political slant go," I had thought. There were so many human stories. Still the political kept thrusting itself in. "Why everything is political up here in the Northwest," a man had told me that day, and, "I guess that's right," I had been compelled to reply. In the hall, at the political meeting, held after the recent election, preparations already being made for the next election, a poet had approached me. He was a poet of the Northwest, or said he was. I doubted it because he wanted to talk to me of the Indians who lived in the Northern forests before the white men, the Swedes, Norskies, Danes, and Finns came in. "There are some beautiful old stories of the Indians a man like you would like to hear," he said, and, "Oh, yeah," I had answered. I wasn't so nice to the poet. I dare say he was on relief.

As for the big farm woman, with the three tickets, I did not speak to her. There had been dozens of just such women present at the other political meetings I had attended. Politics, these political meetings, had obviously taken the place, in part at least, of the church, as the centre of the social life of the country. The women were in it as deeply as the men. I could see that.

It had opened my eyes. In the South, where I had been living for the last several years, politics and political meetings were as yet affairs of the men. In the South and in the rural districts, the men and women got together only at the churches and when they walked to church in single file, the man always headed the procession, the woman and the children at his heels. "I'll bet they don't walk that way up here," I thought.

"Even when they have to wade through the deep snow I'll bet they break a double path."

In the South, and particularly in the country where there are no movies, all of the social life, for young and old, centres about the church, but in the Northwest it is the political meeting that brings them in.

As for the Farmer-Labor movement, there are the two organizations and together they cover Minnesota and are reaching down into Iowa and Wisconsin and into North and South Dakota. The Farmer-Labor Party is political, and the Farmer-Labor Association seems to be primarily an educational effort. The whole movement is partly an outgrowth of the old Non-Partisan League, partly a kind of spontaneous upgrowth out of the soil and of the shops in the towns, and it is partly the result of the long-time effort of old socialists and radicals. The movement has taken different forms in the various states, but in all of them it is essentially the same. There is an association, clubs formed, small dues collected. There is the Farm Holiday Association, The Farmer's Union, The United Farmer's League, and The Farm Bureau. These, on the surface at least, not primarily political—they take in the collectives for buying and selling—but they are used as the foundation for the political movement. In one State the political movement will have captured the old Republican or the Democratic Party, while in another it will have taken a new name, calling itself Progressive or Farmer-Labor. It all seems related, although when you speak to one of the leaders about possible plans for a national third party, he becomes at once noncommital. "It all depends," says the insider.

"Depends upon what?" you ask.

"Why, upon Franklin D. Roosevelt."

At the top the immediate political manifestation, a United States Senator elected or not elected —"He doesn't really represent us just the same" —"He's pretty good"—"He's the best we've got to put up"—the same for a governor or the members of a State legislature. This at the top—the politician with his definite determination to win an election often, in the confusion, controlling. He doesn't always express a deeper restlessness that seems to lie down below, and it is the restlessness you feel in the little meetings, the groping, if you please, willingness to talk, talk, talk. Eagerness to talk. I have been listening to the talk all over the Middlewest, this new hunger for understanding of what government might be, of what it can be, what it is possible to get out of government —a restless growing and determined belief that some kind of a good life is possible for more people through government. The difference between the Northwest and most of the Middlewest being that the Northwest is more ready to throw old-party connections overboard, to form new parties, to go off at almost any experimental tangent. This you do feel in the Northwest and it is the more surprising to you, coming among this people, walking about, looking and listening, because of the nature of the people.

They are on the whole a big-framed and outwardly quiet people, these Danes, Swedes, Norskies, and Finns. There is everywhere among them —I am quite sure this is not the writer's romanticism—less of the American neuroticism, at least outwardly. Who was it spoke up, saying, "Remember the Scandinavian tendency to go somewhere when he does start. Remember the University of Minnesota football team."

At least there was that farm woman, the big one, at the Farmer-Labor meeting in the small town, where I got snowed in, the woman with the tickets on the turkey, the poorly dressed woman who wanted that turkey so desperately. Some one told me of her later. Her husband had died, after losing the farm the pair of them had worked so hard to buy, and he had left her with eight children.

She had rented another farm, had become the farming head of her family. "She's big enough to steer a plow all right," I thought, looking at her. "She should be the mother of strong sons," I also thought, watching her face as the turkey raffle went on. How she did want to win that turkey. "She hasn't raised any turkeys on her own farm," I decided. It would make a royal holiday feast for herself and her children. The raffle came off and she did not win. The big, man-like hand opened when the lucky number was called out and the tickets slid to the floor. I went to stand near her and she was already deep in conversation with another woman. They were on the subject of State taxes.

This, I think, is characteristic of all of these organizations in the Northwest now—they are boldly experimental, willing to take a chance—

they want and will follow bold leaders. Governor Floyd Olson of Minnesota is the type. These people of the North, so many of them with Scandinavian blood in their veins are not scared, as are so many Americans by the words communism or socialism. "Well, what about it?" they say. "Come on. Explain." There are sentences on the lips of men and women. You pick them up everywhere, on the streets and at the meetings they are always holding. "We're up against it. We've got to find a way out. It's our one hope.

"What's the use getting discouraged and giving up because some plan we've tried doesn't work or because some politician sells us out?" Here is the thing you are always hearing talk about in Washington nowadays, that is to say long-time planning, actually got down into the consciousness of people.

"It won't happen today or tomorrow. You've got to plug away at it." These Swedes, Norskies, Danes, Finns, sons and daughters of these men, farmers, some of them small-town store-keepers, keepers of the little taverns in the towns, with whom I have been sitting and talking, all have this new thing in them, oddly mixed—that is to say, it is an odd thing to find in Americans—with patience. It is pretty apparent, I think, that you can't scare them with firecrackers. It should be kept in mind that Floyd Olson, recently re-elected Governor of Minnesota by some seventy thousand votes, was formerly an IWW, a Wobbly. And does he deny it? Not he. I dined with a man who holds an important State office and whose son had, a short time before, been arrested and thrown into jail for taking part in a radical demonstration and was the father ashamed? He laughed when I asked the question. He had a notion, he said, that a boy had to find his own way to his own beliefs.

"All of us older men may be out of it in the end. I don't want my son listening to me. I've slept in too many soft beds," he said.

"You are one of our American writers?" This from the lips of a young student I had met. I had heard that he was one of the brilliant students of one of the smaller colleges of the State. He was curious about me, wondered what sort of a writer I was. He said he had, he thought, heard my name. "I think you must write stories. Yes, now I remember that I have heard you do.

"You see," he said, and I could see that he was in no way apologizing for his ignorance regarding me and my books. "You see I have always been too busy to read any fiction. I have had to work my way through school, and when I am not at work I have to study. If you had spent your life writing about politics and government I would have read your books. I am going in for political economy," he said.

A NORTHWEST LEADER

There is one man who stands out. If you want youth he is young. It is a little hard to guess, after being with the man, how old or how young he is. Let's say he is forty-three, but he might as well be twenty-three or fifty-five. He is a big-boned one, like the farm woman of the turkey raffle. He is big-handed, a mixture of Swede and Dane—I guess it's just as well to be Scandinavian if you want to get along politically in the Northwest— He is a former wandering laborer.

So there it is. He has just the political background America loves. It's all there, city newsboy, clerk, night school education. Hard years are no new thing in the Northwest country so, besides being an itinerant worker in the wheat fields, say in North Dakota, he drifted on West and did a turn as lumberjack in the big woods. That is where he would have got his Wobbly card. There is a lot of the slam and bang and go of the old Western Wobblies in Governor Floyd Olson.

And a lot else, too. Olson is one of the laughing men. When you meet him he'll jump on a table, laugh, size you up, take your measure. "Well, come on then. Let's do it. Let's give it a try." That is his method. To an outsider coming in to this Northwest leader, very curious, talking first, as I did, to a lot of his subordinates and to people met on the streets of Minnesota towns and on Minnesota country roads, to people who have known him since he was a boy——

—He's a lot the boy yet——

—He seems to have known personally every man and woman you meet in Minnesota——

—To an outsider coming in there is something touching about the way the man is loved and believed in. He is like Roosevelt in that, having something of the same quality. He gets under their belts.

"Why you want my notion of Floyd," says the man in the street. They all use his first name. "Say, you can't get it from me. I can't be very clear-headed about that baby. I'm stuck on the man." In the Northwest they are watching their Floyd all right and I rather think they are praying for him.

For the Northwest, with the exception perhaps of South Dakota, is pretty radical. North Dakota and Minnesota are really radical and, as every one

knows, or ought to know, it's a lot easier to be
a successful radical out of office than in.

In the recent election Floyd Olson went in
again and he went in in the face of a kind of conservative revival, the daily newspapers of the
State solidly against him. Of the four hundred
and fifty country weeklies in the State four hundred were also against him.

The small merchants of the towns had quit him.
Two years before he had the small-town merchants solidly behind him because he was then
fighting the chain stores and the Minnesota legislature did try to tax the chain stores out of the
State, but the tax law they passed was declared
unconstitutional and so that didn't go.

And this time—there was the platform. If the
State of Minnesota is radical the platform on
which Olson stood for re-election was more radical. The story they tell is that it was put through,
at the Farmer-Labor Party convention, by a small
group, headed by Howard Y. Williams—Williams being a Minnesota man, former farmer, then
preacher. He had left the State to live in the
East but had come back, sent back by The League
for Independent Political Action, a group headed
by John Dewey and other radical political think-
ers of the East. Williams is also a big and a laugh-

ing man. "He can sure talk the birds down out of the trees," a Farmer-Labor organization man said to me. In the convention he gave the Farmer-Labor Party a platform to stand on that frightened out the small-town merchants—they with visions of having their little stores grabbed by the State—some of the co-operatives and a lot of the farmers.

It was only labor that really stuck and, as with Holt in West Virginia, that put Olson across. The farmers who owned their own farms and who weren't hopelessly in debt at the bank were scared out.

Cries of communism and of socialism. The Farmer-Labor people all said the same thing. "We've been in some hot fighting in some of our other campaigns but this one was a darb." They won with Olson but they did it for the simple reason that so many people of the State love the man and believe in him, but they took the legislature away from him and thus tied his hands.

Did his hands need tying? Did he need to be tied down? At the first meeting with him, when you talk with him, hear him talk, you are inclined to laugh at the notion.

Olson is one of the few men I have met in American political life, and this goes most of all for governors of States, who is not cautious in conversation. He doesn't at all give the impression of being afraid he will be misunderstood or mis-quoted, saying with every breath, every time he begins to really talk, to get down somewhere near the roots—"now be careful—this is off the rec-ords." As for the records he seems constantly to be saying the opposite thing. "All right," he says. "Go ahead. Slap her in."

He is a big laughing man who gives you the impression of being all alive and aware. The aver-age man, at all high in political life, when you speak to him of things you have seen in your wanderings, the farmers really up against it, work-ers in their thousands who hunger for work, the grim fact of youth that sees no future, actual want, plenty of it everywhere—begin to get at these things with the average politician and there comes the queer look of the eyes.

"We ought to have something more than just food for ourselves and the kids in a country like this, and, by Heavens, we're going to have it."

The mutterings that go on, the politician giving lip service to your own aroused feelings. Then fear. Caution. It doesn't seem ever to go down into them, into where they live, as it does into Olson.

You can get at Floyd Olson in that way. He is physically a big blustering fellow, but as you talk with him you feel prayers in him, and not to be sentimental, tears in him.

Olson has been a real worker, he has been through the mill, has lived the rough life with rough men and he hasn't as yet, and in spite of his success in political life, forgotten what the real unrest, the as yet quiet but determined unrest among the farmers and workers of his Northwest is all about. The man knows, he feels, and it is his knowing and feeling that has made him what he is, the outstanding and the best-loved leader of the radical Northwest.

As for the unrest of the Northwest, in Wisconsin apparently going a lot deeper than the La Follettes, as leaders, are willing to go, a lot deeper than the Shipsteads will go, it has a quality unlike any unrest I was able to find in Ohio, Illinois, or Indiana.

It may be because of a difference in the quality of the people themselves—and I think perhaps it is—this touching the industrial labor in the few big towns and spreading far and wide among the farmers—a quality I do not feel expressed in the newspapers or even in the radical press.

It is, I think, the quiet determined thing I have

already mentioned. It is something naïve. It is belief. It does seem, to the outsider coming in, trying only to be reporter, not just trying to write flash, to find the quick obvious drama, to be the thing we are always hearing talk of in the East.

"It would be all right," the East is always saying, "if we could find this impulse—to destroy only what needs destroying and then to build, to make something new—if we could find it as a real American impulse—something not imported, something that is our own."

That is to say a truly determined American thing, not too much hatred, not always thinking of people with their backs to some wall.

This is a kind of ideal you are always hearing talk of in the East. Surely, if it came, it would have in it the thing you find here, in the Northwest, this quiet determination, this patience, this persistent belief that life in America can be made a good life for Americans. The Swedes, Danes, Norskies, and Finns of the Northwest, led by their Floyd Olson may go pretty far. They are determined enough.

What the Woman Said

The Return of the Princess

The Return of the Princess

THE Princess is a big woman. In the last fifteen years she has been in America a good deal, often down on her luck, but she has, except when driven to it, never taken advantage of the fact that she is a princess. She has a quality that few enough people have. She does not live in a dream world. In my conversations with her I have never noticed the peculiar haze, the wall of romantic smoke, that stands between most people and life.

There is the average man or woman walking about. There is a street, or the town or city, in which such a one lives. Let us say that something happens to the street. A row of trees is cut away, there is a fire or a tall building goes up.

There is a startled moment. "Is this the same street in which I have so often walked?"

In a moment there is an adjustment. "Yes. It is the same. Nothing has really happened. There is no change."

What a lie! Everything is constantly changing

but how we all hate to admit change. How eagerly we deny it. We will not accept. "No. No," we cry.

As though these events—the coming of industrialism—the World War—all the tremendous things that have recently happened had made no change in any of our lives. Can Europe, for example, be the same Europe you and I used to visit? Is America the same?

Or this son, who has come home from the wars. "Look, he walks in the same way. The color of his eyes has not changed. Is he the same lad?"

We know he is not. We hope he is. We hate to admit events. Persistently we go on, living in one world and thinking in another. We are all romanticists. "Human nature does not change," we cry, but obviously it is the one thing that does constantly change. Every physical change in the world about me changes me.

The woman was a princess in one of the countries destroyed by the World War. Really it was a civilization that was destroyed. "My title has never been of much real use to me," she once told me.

"Well, yes, it has," she added laughing. "Let us imagine that you sometime take it into your head to write about me. It would be an adventure to have some one write of me. It is one of the adventures I have not had.

"It would give," she said, "a certain fillip to your writing."

"What?" I asked.

"Why—can't you see—that you—who write of the American scene—they expect it of you—that you should write of a princess.

"You live, you see, in a democracy. You hope it is that. You yourself think of yourself as a democrat. Ha! So you are writing, let me say for one of your newspapers, or for a magazine. Aha! You are writing of a princess. These democrats of yours will love that.

"It used to be said," she added, "of the Russians—you scratch a Russian and you will find a Tartar. This is strange, too. The Tartars are very nice people. What if you do find a Tartar?"

The princess became excited. She had already told me of some of her adventures since her return to America. There had been a patent medicine man on a corner, and she had stood listening to his patter. "He was delicious," she said. "He spoke about snakes. He got a salve out of the snakes." She declared that the American crowd, standing and listening to the man, who called himself "Colorado Cal," were amused as she was.

Still they had bought his salve. "Why not?" she said, "I bought some myself."

She had been to Communist meetings and to meetings of the unemployed. There had been a campaign on. She had been to Republican and Democratic speakings, had been to Washington. "Everyday, since I have been here I have walked in the streets looking at people.

"This I will tell you," she cried. "This I must tell you—as you write of me—first of all you must describe me—you will make me a handsome woman—there is something you must say.

"Make me say this—" she made a motion with her hands— "Please, please, you have here, as yet, a democracy. Do not throw it away."

She became more and more excited. "You tell them that—do not become Fascists, you must say to them. Do not ever have a dictator. Do not stir up the race hatreds." It was apparent that the princess was very much in earnest. Her voice trembled. "Do not set up the infallible one, the dictator," she said.

"Please do not do it," she kept saying, over and over.

She said she realized that just now America was not a very happy land. "But in a strange way, in spite of all the injustice that is being done, the injustice to labor, the strikes, men and women are sometimes being beaten and killed in the streets —it is very cruel—formerly I did not know but since I myself have been broke——

"People who once were secure are no longer secure—oh, but here, my dear man, in spite of all—I feel something.

"There is the creeping fear over there," she said. "The creeping fear comes with the dictator."

She explained to me about her title.

"Yes," she said, "I am a real princess. My family had land and estates. We were in a country taken over by the Russians. This was long ago. It was when the Russians, the Prussians, and the Austrians were biting pieces out of Poland. A bite for Russia, a bite for Austria, and then one for Prussia. Soon it was gone. It was swallowed.

"And still," she said, "you see I was of the blood. I was a princess, married to an old prince. And then came the World War.

"And so we were thrown out. We were destroyed. My husband was killed in the war. Huh! What did I care. Have I not told you he was an old man?

"And so I was in Germany, and then in Italy, and then here—in your United States. I made a mistake. I should have stayed here. I was very foolish."

She was in America after the World War and had no money. She thought—"Now I am here in this democracy. I will not say that I have a title."

At that time she was a very handsome woman. Just after the World War she would have been, let us say, a woman of thirty. She spoke several languages.

"I thought I would be a true democrat," she said, "but I could get no work. I wanted to do translations. I wanted to stay here, to be an American.

"And so then, when I could not get any work, when I was broke, I went to a business man. 'I'm a princess,' I said. I proved it to him and immediately he gave me a job. I could see the eyes of the American business man shine. He was a banker and I worked for him for a long time. 'Aha! You see! I have a princess working for me.' Is it not to amuse?

"But, you see, I did not stay. I made a mistake. I fled. I went back to Europe. Oh, how foolish I was. I was thinking, you see, of an old Europe."

She had left America just on the eve of what we all now know as the time of the crash. She left in the fall, a few weeks before it happened. As she talked I remembered having seen her at just that time.

She was about to sail. She had accumulated a little money. She had been working for a banker and he had been giving her tips.

"Although I was working for him—I took care of his correspondence," she at that time explained, "he, this banker—he was fond of taking me out among his friends.

"He did not say to his friends, to those to whom he took me, that I was an employee. Ah! you see. He could not bear it that I, a princess, should be an employee.

"And at the same time, you see, he was proud that I was his employee."

And so he, the banker, had given her tips. When they were alone together in his office she said he called her "the princess."

"Princess," he said, when they were alone together, "here is something that will be good. I will carry a thousand shares of it for you."

She had taken the money got thus, and had gone back to Europe. I remember what she said at that time.

"There is too much prosperity here," she said. I had gone with her, at that time, to the house of a friend. The friend was a poor man. He was a painter.

He was a Polish man painting here and even then and in spite of what seemed, at that time, the almost universal prosperity, every one talking of profits made in stocks, everywhere new American millionaires being made—even then, alas, a good many people were out of work. There was however a sort of glistening golden outer surface to life.

And even then, underneath, through it all, the disease. We call it "over-production." Call it what you will, it was going on then.

The Polish painter, to whose house I went at that time, where I met the princess, not being in on it all. He was living at that time in poverty in two little rooms, on Avenue A in the city of New York, and I remember yet the puzzled look on the face of his thin little wife, and the barren rooms. The paintings he could not sell were piled against the bare walls of the rooms. I remember the talk of the princess at that time, of the vulgarity of our life here. "I cannot stand it," she said.

"Money, money, money," she cried. She spoke of the people she had been meeting. "Aha! Well, I have got some money from them."

She had planned to return to Europe to what she thought of then as an old and a cultured life there. She had this charm of person. I remember yet and sharply how much I liked and admired her on that day.

At that time I had already been with her on another occasion. It was in the city of Washington. It was at the inauguration of a new president. We had together seen that, the foreign woman and myself, the inauguration of an American president.

So there it was. There was the parade, the soldiers marched, the bands played, citizens marched and afterwards—the great weariness of the crowds. She went with me on the night of the inauguration of the American president, to my railroad station. At the station the crowd was milling about.

There were brass bands and all day they had been marching with the political clubs. The big day was at an end. There was the curious weariness of an American crowd, composed of people all of whom had been grimly determined to have a good time . . . this at an end, the weariness—the sadness of it all.

"Look," she said, "it is sad. They do not know how to play."

We were standing there, in that crowd. She

went that night to the leader of one of the bands. "Come on, wake up," she cried. It is but fair to explain that she and I, with others, had had several drinks. This would have been during the time of prohibition. She made the band leader—I remember him as a small man with a gray mustache— he was with a band from some inland town—she made him arouse his band.

At her suggestion the band played a dance piece in the crowded railroad station and turning to a man standing near—he was an American Legion man, an ex-soldier—she made him dance with her. In a few minutes she had every one dancing. "You get a woman and dance with her," she commanded me and when I hesitated she ran and got me one.

"Make them dance. Make every one dance!" she called to the men and women standing about.

And so this woman who had gone home to Europe had come back to us. I dined with her, and she talked. When I saw her recently she had been here for a month. "I am nearly broke," she said. "I am looking for work. I shall have to approach some business man again. I will have to tell him I have a title."

She began to speak of her Europe and of what had happened to her since I had seen her last. "I am so glad to be out of it all, to be here," she said. She had been in Italy, in Russia, in Germany. "There are no smiles over there," she said, "there is no laughter.

"There had been formerly in Europe," she explained, "an old thing—a real culture," she called it. But when men are hungry and desperate there is no culture." She spoke at length of the creeping fear, in Germany, in Italy, in Russia. "There is a kind of madness, the madness of desperation," she declared. "Everywhere there is this cry for the dictator going up. It is in Spain now. I wish that all of you Americans could go and see, could live in one of these countries for a time."

She began telling a long rambling tale. It concerned the queer disappearing of people. This or that man or woman had talked too freely. The man or woman disappears. There is no trial. "They are gone. You do not see them again."

"Any kind of dictator—it does not matter what class in society he represents, or who puts him into power—it is the same thing," she declared.

"There comes the creeping fear. Caution! Caution! Caution!

"Be careful! Please do not talk. It has run all over Europe—the thing—the fear."

My friend, the European woman, is now, alas, what she is. She spoke of that. "I'm no longer young. My beauty has gone.

"But I am again here, in your land. Even though I have a title I am also a woman.

"I am like a man in this—I want to walk freely, to talk," she said. "I do not want to be afraid. I do not want the fear that has run over Europe, that runs over any land to which the dictator comes.

"You in America," she added—she was terribly in earnest now—"began something here. Please, please do not give it up. Formerly, when I was here I did not understand. Do not get the fear over here." In spite of all the depression, she declared that she still found something in America that, compared to Europe, was gay and alive. She had been going about among people. "I have been looking and listening," she said. "I am glad inside. You do not yet have the fear.

"It would be nice," she said, "if you would make me say this.

"But do not make me as I am now. Make me as I was when you saw me first. I was younger then. Make me stand up before the people and cry to them, 'Keep it! Keep it!' Make me say, 'You in America, in spite of all the desperate position you may now be in, may be again what you were. You were once the hope of the world, the place to which the oppressed came. You may be it again.' The fear comes when the dictator comes," she said, again. "There is something you over here do not yet comprehend. It is the creeping fear." She put her face into her hands.

"Keep it! Keep it!" she said again. "The dictator will always betray. He must," she said. "There must be one strong land in the world to which no dictator comes, to which the creeping fear does not come," said the European woman sitting with me at the table in the restaurant with her hands over her eyes.